The Heart
of a
Grandma

365 Days Devotional
for Grandma
Filled with Love, Faith,
and Joy Everyday

A Gift for You

Thank you for choosing this devotional.

To support your journey of faith, we created a special gift bundle for our readers.

Inside the Anchored Grace Reader Gift Bundle, you will receive:

- A free digital devotional

- Printable prayer journal pages

- Scripture reflection cards

- Bonus devotionals for different seasons of life

- Daily encouragement from Anchored Grace

Simply scan the QR code below or visit the link to receive your free bundle.

ddevo.anchoredgraces.com/grandmagift

Scan the QR code with your phone camera or type the link into your browser.

We pray these resources continue to encourage your heart each day.

JANUARY 1

TRUSTING GOD'S FRESH START

"Trust in the Lord with all your heart and lean not on your own understanding; in all your ways acknowledge Him, and He shall direct your paths." **Proverbs 3:5-6**

DEVOTIONAL

To embrace new beginnings is to trust that God has a beautiful plan for us, even when we feel lost or alone.

What new beginnings might God be inviting you to embrace in this season of your life? How can you trust Him more fully as you step into these opportunities?

PRAYER

Dear Lord, thank You for the gift of new beginnings. Help me to trust in Your plan and to embrace the fresh starts You provide each day.

Every dawn is an invitation to rise anew, leaving yesterday behind and stepping boldly into God's grace.

JANUARY 2

SHARING LIFE LESSONS

"She opens her mouth with wisdom, and the teaching of kindness is on her tongue." **Proverbs 31:26**

DEVOTIONAL

Never underestimate the power of your words; they can be the very seeds of wisdom that nurture the next generation.

What life lesson do you cherish and wish to share with those you love most? How can you weave this wisdom into your conversations and moments together?

PRAYER

Dear Lord, thank you for the wisdom you've granted us through our experiences. Help us to share our lessons with love and grace, guiding those we cherish on their journeys.

Sharing wisdom is like planting seeds; you never know when they will bloom.

JANUARY 3

EMBRACING CHANGE IN THE NEW YEAR

"She is clothed with strength and dignity; she can laugh at the days to come." **Proverbs 31:25**

DEVOTIONAL

Change, like a new quilt, may seem daunting at first, but it often reveals a tapestry of unforeseen beauty and connection.

What changes do you feel God inviting you to embrace in this new year, and how can you open your heart to those opportunities?

PRAYER

Dear God, as we step into this new year, grant us the courage to embrace change with grace. Help us recognize Your hand in every transition and trust that your plans are good. Amen.

Like the seasons that turn, we too can find beauty in the changes of life.

JANUARY 4

PRAYING FOR OUR FAMILIES

"Do not be anxious about anything, but in every situation, by prayer and petition, with thanksgiving, present your requests to God." **Philippians 4:6-7**

DEVOTIONAL

We may not always be able to solve our family's problems, but we can faithfully lift them up to the Lord in prayer, trusting His perfect plan.

What are the specific needs and challenges your family faces that you can lift up in prayer today? How can you draw closer to God as you bring these concerns before Him?

PRAYER

Dear Lord, thank You for the gift of family. Help me to cover them in prayer daily and trust in Your perfect will for their lives.

Great love is often expressed in quiet prayers.

JANUARY 5

THE BLESSING OF GRANDCHILDREN

"Children's children are a crown to the aged, and parents are the pride of their children." **Proverbs 17:6**

DEVOTIONAL

The blessings of grandchildren remind us that life is filled with opportunities for connection, joy, and the endless sharing of love across generations.

What do you cherish most about the moments you've spent with your grandchildren, and how do these memories fill your heart with joy?

PRAYER

Dear Lord, thank You for the precious gift of grandchildren. May the time spent with them be filled with love and laughter, and may I always share Your wisdom and warmth with each cherished moment.

Grandchildren are not just a part of our legacy; they are the joy that colors our days.

JANUARY 6

FINDING JOY IN SIMPLE MOMENTS

"Rejoice in the Lord always. I will say it again: Rejoice!" **Philippians 4:4**

DEVOTIONAL

In the tapestry of life, the most vibrant threads come from moments of connection and joy found in the ordinary.

What simple moment in your day brings you the most joy, and how can you cherish it more fully?

PRAYER

Dear Lord, thank you for the gift of simple moments in our lives. Help us to recognize and embrace these joys, filling our hearts with gratitude.

Joy often hides in the small, ordinary moments we may overlook.

JANUARY 7

RENEWING BODY AND SPIRIT

"Come to me, all you who are weary and burdened,
and I will give you rest." Matthew 11:28

DEVOTIONAL

In our seasons of life, it's vital to carve out time for ourselves in the midst
of our caring roles, for even the most devoted caregivers need moments of
peace to rejuvenate.

*What activities bring you a sense of peace and rest? How can you intentionally
carve out time for these moments in your week?*

PRAYER

Dear Lord, thank You for the gift of rest. Help me to embrace the stillness
of the Sabbath, renewing both my body and spirit in Your presence.

True rest is not merely the absence of activity,
but the presence of peace.

JANUARY 8

PASSING DOWN TRADITIONS

"Train up a child in the way he should go; even when he is old he will not
depart from it." Proverbs 22:6

DEVOTIONAL

The sweetest gifts we can pass down to our grandchildren are the
traditions and stories that make our families unique.

*What traditions have you cherished and passed down to your family? How do these
customs shape the bonds you share with your loved ones?*

PRAYER

Dear Lord, thank You for the beautiful traditions that weave our families
together. Help us to honor and preserve these legacies, sharing love and
wisdom with each generation.

Traditions are the threads that connect our past with our future.

One Week Together

You've just completed your first week of devotionals.

If these reflections have brought peace or encouragement into your day, would you consider sharing a short Amazon review?

devo.anchoredgraces.com/grandma

Your words help other women discover devotionals that may support them on their own faith journey.

Thank you for spending these moments in reflection.

JANUARY 9

THE POWER OF ENCOURAGEMENT

"Anxiety weighs down the heart, but a kind word cheers it up."
Proverbs 12:25

DEVOTIONAL

Never underestimate the significance of a kind word; your encouragement can uplift a weary heart and change someone's day.

What words of encouragement have you shared with someone recently? How did it make you feel, and how did it impact their day?

PRAYER

Dear Lord, thank you for the gift of encouragement. Help us to uplift those around us with kind words and heartfelt support, just as you uplift us.

Your words can be the sunshine for someone's cloudy day.

JANUARY 10

GOD'S FAITHFULNESS THROUGH GENERATIONS

"For the Lord is good; His steadfast love endures forever, and His faithfulness to all generations." **Psalm 100:5**

DEVOTIONAL

Our stories of faith are gifts we can pass down, demonstrating how God's faithfulness sustains us and shapes our family legacy.

What stories of God's faithfulness have you seen unfold in your family over the years? How have those experiences shaped your understanding of His love?

PRAYER

Dear Lord, thank You for Your unwavering faithfulness through all generations. Help us to continue sharing Your love and grace with our families, that they may also know Your presence in their lives.

Faithfulness is a gentle thread woven through
the fabric of our family history.

NURTURING FRIENDSHIPS IN LATER LIFE

"Two are better than one, because they have a good reward for their toil; for if they fall, one will lift up his fellow." **Ecclesiastes 4:9-10**

DEVOTIONAL

Friendship is a beautiful tapestry, stitched together with love, laughter, and shared experiences, especially in these later years where we find strength in each other.

What does friendship mean to you in this season of your life, and how can you invest in those special connections with the people around you?

PRAYER

Dear Lord, help me cherish the friendships I have and seek new connections that bring joy and support. Grant me the wisdom to nurture these bonds with love and kindness.

Friendships are the heart's garden; they flourish with care and love.

JANUARY 12

SERVING OTHERS WITH A GRATEFUL HEART

"Let each of you look not only to his own interests, but also to the interests of others." **Philippians 2:4**

DEVOTIONAL

The joy of serving others is magnified in our hearts when we approach it with gratitude, for it reminds us of the blessings we have to share.

What are the simple acts of kindness you can offer to those around you today, and how might you express your gratitude in those moments?

PRAYER

Dear Lord, thank you for the gift of service and the joy it brings. Help me to see opportunities to lend a hand and share love with others, filled with a grateful heart.

Gratitude opens the door to a heart that serves.

JANUARY 13

THE COMFORT OF GOD'S PRESENCE

"Where can I go from Your Spirit? Or where can I flee from Your presence? If I ascend to heaven, You are there; if I make my bed in hell, behold, You are there. If I take the wings of the morning and dwell in the uttermost parts of the sea, even there Your hand shall lead me, and Your right hand shall hold me." **Psalm 139:7-10**

DEVOTIONAL
In the quiet moments of your life, remember that God's presence is always with you, a gentle reminder of love and comfort.

What moments in your daily life remind you of God's comforting presence? How can you seek that presence in times of uncertainty?

PRAYER
Dear Lord, thank you for your unwavering presence in our lives. May we always feel your comforting touch and find peace in your love. Amen.

In the quiet moments of our days,
God's presence whispers love and reassurance.

JANUARY 14

EMBRACING GRACE FOR OURSELVES

"And after you have suffered a little while, the God of all grace, who has called you to his eternal glory in Christ, will himself restore, confirm, strengthen, and establish you." **1 Peter 5:10**

DEVOTIONAL
Embracing grace means allowing ourselves the freedom to begin again, knowing that our worth is not defined by our successes or failures.

What does it mean for you to truly embrace grace in your own life, allowing forgiveness and love to flow not just to others, but also to yourself? How might this understanding transform your everyday moments?

PRAYER
Dear Lord, thank You for the gift of grace that surrounds us each day. Help us to accept Your love and to share it with ourselves, so we can live fully in joy and peace.

Embracing grace means recognizing
the beautiful worth in our imperfections.

JANUARY 15

JUSTICE & KINDNESS

"And do not forget to do good and to share with others, for with such sacrifices God is pleased." Hebrews 13:16

DEVOTIONAL

In our golden years, let us continue to share our love and compassion with others, knowing that our actions can change lives.

What are some ways you can embody the spirit of justice and kindness in your daily life, especially in your interactions with family and friends?

PRAYER

Dear God, thank You for the legacy and for reminding us of the importance of justice and kindness. Help us to reflect Your love in our actions and be a beacon of hope in our communities.

Kindness is a quiet strength that changes hearts.

JANUARY 16

FINDING PURPOSE IN RETIREMENT

"Delight yourself in the LORD, and He will give you the desires of your heart." Psalm 37:4

DEVOTIONAL

In retirement, it's never too late to cultivate new passions and share your gifts with others.

What activities or passions have you set aside during your busy years that now spark excitement as you enter this new season of life? How might God be inviting you to explore these deeper?

PRAYER

Dear Lord, thank you for the gift of this new chapter in my life. Help me to discover and embrace the purpose you have for me in my retirement, filling my days with joy and meaningful service.

Retirement is not the end of an era, but the beginning of an adventure.

JANUARY 17

GOD'S CREATION

"The grass withers, and the flowers fade, but the word of our God remains forever." Isaiah 40:8

DEVOTIONAL

Embrace the beauty of each season in life, knowing that even in winter, God's grace surrounds us, bringing warmth and joy.

What does the beauty of winter remind you about God's faithfulness in your life? How can you embrace this season of rest and reflection?

PRAYER

Dear God, thank you for the beauty of winter and the quiet moments it brings. Help me to see your hand in every snowflake and to find joy in the stillness of this season.

In the quiet of winter, God whispers His love, inviting us to pause and reflect on the beauty around us.

JANUARY 18

PRAYING FOR OUR NATION

"And my people, who are called by my name, humble themselves and pray and seek my face and turn from their wicked ways, then I will hear from heaven and will forgive their sin and heal their land." 2 Chronicles 7:14

DEVOTIONAL

Our prayers can create ripples of hope and change, stirring the hearts and minds of those who govern and guide our nation.

What specific concerns do you have for our nation that you can bring to God in prayer today? Take a moment to reflect on how these worries connect to your heart and experiences.

PRAYER

Dear Heavenly Father, we come before you with hearts heavy for our nation. Guide our leaders and fill us with the courage to be voices of love and unity. Help us to continue to pray diligently for the peace and well-being of our land.

Prayer is our bridge to hope, even when the path seems uncertain.

LETTING GO OF WORRY

"Therefore do not worry about tomorrow, for tomorrow will worry about itself. Each day has enough trouble of its own." Matthew 6:34

DEVOTIONAL

Letting go of worry allows us to embrace the joys of today, nurturing love and connection in every moment.

"What worries have been weighing on your heart lately? Can you take a moment to release them into God's care and trust that He holds your path?

PRAYER

Dear Lord, we come before you with our worries, asking for your peace to fill our hearts. Help us to lean on your strength and let go of the burdens that keep us awake at night. Thank you for your love and guidance.

Worry doesn't empty tomorrow of its sorrow;
it empties today of its strength.

JANUARY 20

THE STRENGTH OF A PRAYING GRANDMOTHER

"Therefore I tell you, whatever you ask in prayer, believe that you have received it, and it will be yours." Mark 11:24

DEVOTIONAL

Prayers offered in love can ignite hope and healing, bridging generational gaps with divine grace.

What has your prayer life looked like this week, and in what ways have you felt God's presence in your conversations with Him?

PRAYER

Dear God, thank You for the gift of prayer and the loving hearts of grandmothers everywhere. Help us to trust in Your power as we lift our families to You each day.

Your prayers are a fabric woven with love,
surrounding your family with warmth and strength.

CHERISHING FAMILY MEMORIES

"Even to your old age and gray hairs I am he, I am he who will sustain you. I have made you and I will carry you; I will sustain you and I will rescue you." Isaiah 46:4

DEVOTIONAL

Our family stories, shared in love, are treasures that bind generations together.

What cherished family memory brings a smile to your face when you think about it? How can you share that joy with your loved ones today?

PRAYER

Dear Lord, thank You for the gift of family and the precious memories we create together. Help us to cherish each moment and pass down the love that binds us through the generations.

Memories are the threads that weave our families together.

GOD'S PROMISES FOR THE FUTURE

"For I know the plans I have for you, declares the Lord, plans to prosper you and not to harm you, plans to give you hope and a future." Jeremiah 29:11

DEVOTIONAL

Even in times of uncertainty, God's promises remind us that we are never alone and that a beautiful future is being cultivated just for us.

What dreams or hopes do you hold for the future that you can entrust to God's loving care?

PRAYER

Heavenly Father, thank You for the promises You have made for our future. Help me to lean into these truths and trust that You are guiding my path with love and wisdom.

Tomorrow holds the beauty of God's faithfulness, waiting to unfold in ways we cannot yet imagine.

Three Weeks of Reflection

You've now spent several weeks walking through these devotionals.

If this book has encouraged your heart, a brief Amazon review helps other women find the same encouragement.

devo.anchoredgraces.com/grandma

Your experience may guide someone else toward the hope they are searching for.

Thank you for being here.

JANUARY 23

THE JOY OF GIVING

"The generous will themselves be blessed,
for they share their food with the poor." **Proverbs 22:9**

DEVOTIONAL

In giving, we discover the true richness of our own hearts, filling them with joy and connection.

What special way can you share your love and resources with those around you today? How can your acts of kindness spark joy in both your heart and theirs?

PRAYER

Dear Lord, thank You for the gift of giving. Help me find joy in sharing my blessings and spreading Your love to everyone I meet.

True joy is found not in what we have, but in what we share.

JANUARY 24

STAYING CONNECTED WITH LOVED ONES

"A friend loves at all times, and a brother is born for a time of adversity."
Proverbs 17:17

DEVOTIONAL

Cherish and nurture your connections, for they are the cherished threads binding your heart to your loved ones.

What ways can you reach out to your loved ones this week, and how will you create moments of connection amidst your busy life?

PRAYER

Dear Lord, thank You for the gift of family and friends. Help me to cherish these connections and foster love in every moment we share. May I reach out with kindness and joy in my heart.

Love grows when nurtured, and every phone call or letter is a seed planted in the hearts of those we cherish.

THE BLESSING OF GOOD HEALTH

"Beloved, I pray that you may prosper in all things and be in health, just as your soul prospers." 3 John 1:2

DEVOTIONAL

Our health is not just our physical strength, but also the energy we bring to our loved ones, allowing us to create beautiful memories together.

What does good health mean to you in this season of your life, and how do you see it as a blessing to share with your family?

PRAYER

Dear Lord, thank You for the gift of health. May I cherish my well-being and use it to bring joy and love to those around me.

Health is not just the absence of illness;
it's the presence of vitality to enjoy every moment.

TRUSTING GOD WITH OUR CONCERNS

"Do not fear, for I am with you; do not be dismayed, for I am your God. I will strengthen you and help you; I will uphold you with my righteous right hand." Isaiah 41:10

DEVOTIONAL

Trusting God means releasing our concerns and believing He is weaving the threads of our family's stories with love and purpose.

What are the concerns that seem to weigh heavily on your heart today, and how can you bring them to God in trust?

PRAYER

Dear Lord, as we gather our thoughts and worries, help us to lay them before You with unwavering trust. May Your peace wash over us, reminding us that we are never alone in our struggles.

Trusting God transforms our worries into whispers of hope.

THE GIFT OF LAUGHTER

"A joyful heart is good medicine, but a crushed spirit dries up the bones."
Proverbs 17:22

DEVOTIONAL

Let laughter fill your heart and home; it is a reminder that joy can thrive even in the simplest moments.

What moments today have brought a smile to your face, and how can you share that laughter with others in your life?

PRAYER

Dear Lord, thank You for the gift of laughter and the joy it brings. Help us to find humor in our days and share that warmth with those around us.

Laughter is a gentle reminder that joy
can be found even in life's smallest moments.

FINDING PEACE IN UNCERTAINTY

"Peace I leave with you; my peace I give you. I do not give to you as the world gives. Do not let your hearts be troubled and do not be afraid."
John 14:27

DEVOTIONAL

Trust that, like the flowers of the garden, your family will thrive in their own time, and let God's peace wash over you in moments of uncertainty.

What uncertainties are weighing on your heart today, and how can you invite peace into those moments?

PRAYER

Dear Lord, as I navigate these uncertain times, help me find comfort in Your presence. Fill my heart with peace and let my trust in You grow deeper each day.

Amid the storms of life, peace can bloom like a flower in the desert.

JANUARY 29

THE IMPORTANCE OF FORGIVENESS

"Be kind to one another, tenderhearted, forgiving one another, as God in Christ forgave you." **Ephesians 4:32**

DEVOTIONAL

The grace of forgiveness can bring healing and connection, lighting the way for deeper family bonds in our golden years.

What memories or hurts from your past do you feel ready to release today in order to embrace a more peaceful heart? How might forgiving someone, even just in your thoughts, lighten your spirit?

PRAYER

Dear Lord, help me to let go of the burdens I carry. Grant me the strength to forgive those who have hurt me, just as You forgive me every day. May Your love fill my heart and guide my actions.

Forgiveness is the gentle act of releasing ourselves from the chains of the past.

JANUARY 30

CELEBRATING MILESTONES

"Every good and perfect gift is from above, coming down from the Father of the heavenly lights, who does not change like shifting shadows." **James 1:17**

DEVOTIONAL

Every milestone is an opportunity to reflect on God's faithfulness and to celebrate the love that connects us across the ages.

What milestones in your life bring you the greatest joy and how can you celebrate them with gratitude today?

PRAYER

Dear Lord, thank you for the beautiful journey of life and the milestones that enrich it. Help me to cherish each moment, celebrating the gifts of family, love, and faith.

Every milestone is a reminder of God's faithful presence through the years.

HOPE FOR THE YEAR AHEAD

"But those who hope in the Lord will renew their strength. They will soar on wings like eagles; they will run and not grow weary, they will walk and not be faint." Isaiah 40:31

DEVOTIONAL

In life, just as in gardening, the promise of hope lies in the ability to persevere and nurture what seems lost, trusting that new beginnings are always possible.

What hopes and dreams do you carry in your heart for the year ahead? How can you take even small steps toward them? Reflect on what brings you joy and how you can invite more of that into your life.

PRAYER

Dear Lord, as I step into this new year, help me to embrace hope and joy in every moment. May my heart be open to your blessings and the potential that each day holds.

Hope lights the path ahead, reminding us
that every new season brings fresh opportunities.

THE WARMTH OF GOD'S LOVE IN WINTER

"When you pass through the waters, I will be with you; and when you pass through the rivers, they will not sweep over you. When you walk through the fire, you will not be burned; the flames will not set you ablaze."
Isaiah 43:2

DEVOTIONAL

In the coldest seasons of life, God's love is like a warm quilt, ready to wrap you up and keep you snug.

What are some ways you can recognize and embrace God's love in the chilly moments of winter? How can this love warm your heart and the hearts of those around you?

PRAYER

Dear Lord, thank You for the warmth of Your love that surrounds us, even in the coldest seasons. Help us to feel Your presence daily and to share that warmth with others. Amen.

In the stillness of winter,
God's love is the gentle fire that burns within us.

TRUSTING GOD'S TIMING

"In their hearts, humans plan their course, but the Lord establishes their steps." **Proverbs 16:9**

DEVOTIONAL

Trusting God's timing can reveal blessings that we may not see in the moment.

What are some areas in your life where you are waiting for God's timing? How can you actively trust Him in that waiting season?

PRAYER

Dear Lord, thank You for being present with us in every season of our lives. Help us to trust in Your perfect timing, knowing that You are always working things out for our good.

Sometimes, the waiting is just as important as the receiving.

THE POWER OF A GENTLE WORD

"A gentle answer turns away wrath, but a harsh word stirs up anger."
Proverbs 15:1

DEVOTIONAL

The most powerful gift we can offer our loved ones is not just our wisdom, but our gentle words that bring healing and support.

What gentle words have you spoken recently that may have lifted someone's spirit? How can you be more intentional in offering kindness through your words today?

PRAYER

Dear Lord, thank you for the power of our words. Help us to speak gently and wisely, sharing your love and encouragement with everyone we meet.

A gentle word can soften even the hardest heart.

PRAYING FOR OUR CHILDREN'S MARRIAGES

"He who finds a wife finds what is good and receives favor from the Lord."
Proverbs 18:22

DEVOTIONAL

As grandmothers, the love we pour into our prayers can become a gentle balm for our children's marriages, nurturing their relationships with the grace and wisdom we've gained over the years.

What specific qualities do you hope for in your children's marriages, and how can your prayers help nurture those desires?

PRAYER

Dear Lord, please bless my children's marriages with love, patience, and understanding. Guide them through the challenges they may face and strengthen their bond each day.

Prayer is the bridge that connects our hopes
for our children to God's heart for their marriages.

THE GIFT OF FRIENDSHIP

"I no longer call you servants, because a servant does not know his master's business. Instead, I have called you friends, for everything that I learned from my Father I have made known to you." John 15:15

DEVOTIONAL

True friendship, like a well-tended garden, brings beauty, joy, and support to our lives, reminding us that we are never alone.

What does friendship mean to you at this stage of your life, and how have your cherished connections shaped who you are today?

PRAYER

Dear Lord, thank you for the precious gift of friendship. Help us nurture these bonds with love and laughter, and remind us of the joy that comes from sharing our lives with others.

Friendship is the thread that weaves our lives together, creating a tapestry rich in love and memories.

FINDING BEAUTY IN THE ORDINARY

"See, I am doing a new thing! Now it springs up; do you not perceive it? I am making a way in the wilderness and streams in the wasteland." Isaiah 43:19

DEVOTIONAL

Sometimes, all we need to do is pause and observe the world around us to find the beauty that is present in the ordinary.

What simple moments in your daily life bring you joy and remind you of the beauty that surrounds you?

PRAYER

Dear Lord, thank You for the everyday wonders that fill our lives with joy. Help me to open my eyes and heart to the beauty in the ordinary moments, letting them deepen my faith and gratitude.

Beauty often lies in the details we overlook—a soft breeze, the laughter of children, or a quiet cup of tea on a sunny afternoon.

FEBRUARY 7

THE BLESSING OF A LOVING HOME

"The Lord s curse is on the house of the wicked, but he blesses the home of the righteous." **Proverbs 3:33**

DEVOTIONAL

True blessings flourish in a home filled with love, where open hearts and open doors welcome all who enter.

What are the ways you feel God's love reflected in your home and family relationships? How can you nurture that blessing further?

PRAYER

Dear Lord, thank you for the gift of family and the warmth of a loving home. Help us to cherish these moments and spread your love within our hearts and into the lives of those around us.

A loving home is a reflection of God's grace,
a sanctuary where hearts are nurtured and love flourishes.

FEBRUARY 8

SHARING FAITH STORIES WITH GRANDCHILDREN

"One generation commends your works to another; they tell of your mighty acts." **Psalm 145:4**

DEVOTIONAL

Every story shared is a thread woven into the fabric of our grandchildren's faith, teaching them that they are part of a God-written legacy.

What stories of faith do you cherish most, and how can you share them in a way that your grandchildren will understand and connect with?

PRAYER

Dear Lord, may the stories of Your love and faithfulness flow from my heart to my grandchildren's ears. Help me to share with joy, wisdom, and grace as we connect through these precious moments.

Faith is a legacy, best shared through the warmth of our stories.

FEBRUARY 9

THE JOY OF COOKING FOR FAMILY

"She rises while it is yet night and provides food for her household and portions for her maidens. She considers a field and buys it; with the fruit of her hands, she plants a vineyard." **Proverbs 31:15-16**

DEVOTIONAL

Cooking for family is not just about nourishing their bodies; it's about weaving together moments of love and connection that create lasting memories.

What is one special dish you can make for your family that brings back cherished memories for you? How does preparing this meal make you feel connected to your loved ones?

PRAYER

Dear Lord, thank you for the gift of family and the joy of cooking. May each meal we prepare be seasoned with love and sprinkled with laughter, nourishing not just our bodies but also our hearts.

Cooking is an act of love that brings generations together, creating bonds that last beyond the dinner table.

FEBRUARY 10

GOD'S LOVE NEVER FAILS

"So we have come to know and to believe the love that God has for us."
1 John 4:16

DEVOTIONAL

Remember, dear ones, that no matter the trials you face, God's love never fails and always nourishes the roots of hope in your heart.

What moments in your life have you felt the unwavering presence of God's love, even amid challenges or uncertainty? How can you carry this love into your relationships with your family and friends?

PRAYER

Dear Lord, thank You for Your steadfast love that guides us each day. Help us to feel Your presence in our hearts and share that love generously with those around us. Amen.

Even in life's storms, God's love is our anchor, holding us firm and steady.

PREPARING OUR HEARTS FOR VALENTINE'S DAY

"And this is my prayer: that your love may abound more and more in knowledge and depth of insight, so that you may be able to discern what is best..." **Philippians 1:9-10**

DEVOTIONAL

Love is a gift we can choose to nurture in our families, enriching both their lives and our own.

What does love mean to you in this season of your life, and how can you express that love to those around you this Valentine's Day? Consider the little ways you can share your heart with family and friends.

PRAYER

Heavenly Father, as Valentine's Day approaches, help us to open our hearts to love in all its beautiful forms. May we cherish the relationships we have and seek to brighten the lives of those we encounter.

True love blossoms in the smallest acts of kindness.

ACTS OF KINDNESS

"A generous person will prosper; whoever refreshes others will be refreshed." **Proverbs 11:25**

DEVOTIONAL

In kindness, we find the joy of connection, reminding us of the love that binds generations together.

What small act of kindness could you offer today that would bring a smile to someone's face or lighten their load? Think about a neighbor, a family member, or even a stranger you might encounter. How can you share your warmth and wisdom with them?

PRAYER

Dear Lord, thank You for the gift of kindness that flows from our hearts. Help us to be instruments of Your love, sharing small gestures that can make a big difference in the world. Amen.

Kindness is the language the deaf can hear and the blind can see.

REMEMBERING LOVED ONES WHO'VE PASSED

"The righteous perishes, and no one lays it to heart; the devout are taken away, and no one understands. That the righteous are taken away to be spared from evil." Isaiah 57:1-2

DEVOTIONAL

Cherish the memories of your loved ones; they are forever a part of your heart's garden.

What cherished memories do you hold of the loved ones you have lost, and how do those memories shape who you are today?

PRAYER

Dear Lord, thank you for the precious gift of our memories. May we find comfort in remembering our loved ones and joy in the legacy of love they left behind.

Even in their absence, the love we shared remains a guiding light in our hearts.

FEBRUARY 14

LOVE THAT LASTS

"Love is patient, love is kind. It does not envy, it does not boast, it is not proud. It does not dishonor others, it is not self-seeking, it is not easily angered, it keeps no record of wrongs. Love does not delight in evil but rejoices with the truth. It always protects, always trusts, always hopes, always perseveres." 1 Corinthians 13:4-7

DEVOTIONAL

True love is not defined by grand gestures but is nurtured in the everyday moments of patience, kindness, and shared laughter.

What does lasting love look like in your life, and how can you share that love with those around you today? How have you seen love endure through the seasons of life?

PRAYER

Dear Lord, thank You for the gift of love that surrounds us and sustains us. Help us to cherish and nurture the relationships that mean the most, reflecting Your everlasting love in all we do.

True love is not just a feeling; it is a commitment that grows deeper with every shared moment.

FEBRUARY 15

THE GIFT OF A LOVING SPOUSE

"For where your treasure is, there your heart will be also."
Matthew 6:21

DEVOTIONAL

True love is a treasure that deepens with each passing year, reminding us to embrace every shared moment with gratitude.

What are some of the cherished moments you've shared with your spouse that make your heart smile?

PRAYER

Dear Lord, thank You for the gift of love we share in our marriages. Help us to appreciate the small moments and to nurture that love each day.

Love is not just in the grand gestures,
but in the quiet moments spent together.

FEBRUARY 16

PRAYING FOR GRANDCHILDREN'S FRIENDSHIPS

"I thank my God every time I remember you."
Philippians 1:3

DEVOTIONAL

Your prayers for your grandchildren are powerful and can shape their lives in ways you may never fully see.

What qualities do you hope your grandchildren seek in their friendships, and how can you gently guide them towards these values?

PRAYER

Dear Lord, I lift my grandchildren up to You, asking for Your guidance in their friendships. May they find companions who uplift and encourage them, and may Your love shine through them in all their interactions.

Friends are the mirrors reflecting our values;
may they reflect kindness, loyalty, and warmth.

THE COMFORT OF GOD'S WORD

"My comfort in my suffering is this: Your promise preserves my life."
Psalm 119:50

DEVOTIONAL

In God's Word, we find the comfort that gently cradles our hearts through every season of life.

What verses from God's Word have brought you comfort in times of trouble, and how can you share those with someone in need today?

PRAYER

Dear Lord, I thank You for the gift of Your Word that guides and comforts me. Please help me to find peace in Your promises and to share that peace with those around me.

In every season of life, God's Word
remains a steady anchor for our hearts.

THE JOY OF FAMILY GATHERINGS

"Behold, children are a heritage from the LORD, the fruit of the womb a reward." **Psalm 127:3**

DEVOTIONAL

In every gathering, may we treasure the love and laughter that surrounds us, for these moments are God's sweetest gifts to our hearts.

What memories do you cherish most from family gatherings, and how do they fill your heart with joy today?

PRAYER

Dear Lord, thank you for the gift of family and the joy that comes from gathering together. Help us to cherish these moments, filling our hearts with love and laughter. Amen.

Family gatherings are the threads that weave the fabric of our hearts.

PRAYING FOR LEADERS

"The king's heart is in the hand of the Lord, like the rivers of water; He turns it wherever He wishes." **Proverbs 21:1**

DEVOTIONAL

As grandmothers, let us remember that our humble prayers can be a powerful source of change and unity, reminding us that we are all part of something greater.

What does family mean to you, and how do you feel God's presence during your family gatherings?

PRAYER

Dear Lord, thank you for the gift of family. May our gatherings be filled with love, laughter, and a sense of Your presence, reminding us of the beauty of togetherness.

Family is the heart of our joy, where love multiplies and memories are woven together.

THE BLESSING OF GOOD NEIGHBORS

"As iron sharpens iron, so one person sharpens another."
Proverbs 27:17

DEVOTIONAL

Remember, dear ones, it is in nurturing our relationships with neighbors that we find true joy and support in life's journey.

What qualities do your neighbors possess that enrich your life, and how might you show appreciation for them today?

PRAYER

Dear Lord, thank you for the neighbors you've placed in my life. Help me to cherish our connections and to share kindness with those living close by.

Good neighbors are like a cozy blanket, providing warmth and comfort in our daily lives.

FEBRUARY 21

FINDING GOD IN QUIET MOMENTS

"Be still, and know that I am God."
Psalm 46:10

DEVOTIONAL

In every quiet moment, God whispers reassurance, inviting us to seek His presence amidst our busy lives.

What are some quiet moments in your day where you feel God's presence most closely, and how can you nurture those moments more intentionally?

PRAYER

Dear Lord, thank you for the quiet moments when we can feel You near. May we find peace in these still times and let Your love fill our hearts.

In the stillness, God whispers His love
and grace, inviting us to draw near.

FEBRUARY 22

THE IMPORTANCE OF LISTENING

"If one gives an answer before he hears, it is his folly and shame."
Proverbs 18:13

DEVOTIONAL

Take a moment to listen fully; it strengthens bonds and brings joy, not just to those who share their stories but to your heart as well.

What is one moment recently where you felt truly heard and how did it impact you?

PRAYER

Dear Lord, thank You for the gift of listening and for the ears You've given us to hear each other. Help us to engage deeply with those around us and reflect Your loving attentiveness in our conversations.

Listening is a sacred act; it allows us to touch the hearts of others.

THE GIFT OF LAUGHTER WITH FRIENDS

"There is a time for everything, and a season for every activity under the heavens: a time to weep and a time to laugh." Ecclesiastes 3:4

DEVOTIONAL

Cherish the gift of laughter with friends, for it adds richness to our days and strengthens our spirits.

What brings you the most joy when you share laughter with your friends? Can you recall a moment recently that filled your heart with joy and connected you all?

PRAYER

Dear Lord, thank You for the gift of laughter and the beautiful friends You've placed in our lives. May we continue to cherish these moments and deepen our connections through joy and love.

Laughter is a thread that weaves together the fabric of friendship.

FEBRUARY 24

PRAYING FOR FAMILY UNITY

Blessed are the peacemakers, for they will be called children of God.
Matthew 5:9

DEVOTIONAL

By nurturing a spirit of love and patience, we can gently guide our families towards harmony amidst life's little squabbles.

What steps can you take today to nurture unity within your family, even when differences arise? Consider how your own heart can open the door to love and understanding.

PRAYER

Dear Lord, may Your peace flow through our family, knitting our hearts together in love and harmony. Guide us in our conversations and actions, fostering unity that reflects Your grace.

True strength in family comes not from our similarities, but from our love that embraces our differences.

FEBRUARY 25

THE STRENGTH TO PERSEVERE

"I can do all things through Christ who strengthens me."
Philippians 4:13

DEVOTIONAL

In life's trials, the love and faith we nurture can transform our struggles into beautiful stories of perseverance.

What challenges in your life require the strength to persevere, and how can you lean on your faith to navigate them? Think about the moments you felt like giving up and the reasons you chose to keep going.

PRAYER

Dear Lord, thank you for every moment of strength you've granted us. Please grant us the wisdom and perseverance to navigate our daily challenges. May we always feel Your presence guiding us through tough times.

Perseverance is the quiet strength that blooms in the soul, reminding us that every season of struggle carries the promise of renewal.

FEBRUARY 26

THE BEAUTY OF FORGIVENESS

"I, even I, am he who blots out your transgressions for my own sake and remembers your sins no more." **Isaiah 43:25**

DEVOTIONAL

In the journey of our lives, the beauty of forgiveness not only heals old wounds but also opens up new paths for love and connection.

What does forgiveness mean to you in your life journey, and how has it shaped your relationships with those you love? Have you found moments where letting go has brought you peace?

PRAYER

Dear Lord, thank You for the gift of forgiveness. Help us to open our hearts and extend grace to those who have hurt us, just as You have extended Your love and mercy to us.

Forgiveness is the gentle balm that soothes the heart, restoring joy and connection in our lives.

THE BLESSING OF A NEW GRANDCHILD

"And when Esau looked up and saw the women and children, he said, 'Who are these with you?' Jacob said, 'The children God has graciously given your servant." **Genesis 33:5**

DEVOTIONAL

Every new grandchild is a precious gift, a special reminder that God's blessings continue to unfold in our lives, often in ways we least expect.

What joys and hopes do you hold in your heart as you welcome this new grandchild into your family? How do you see this little one bringing fresh blessings to your life and the lives of those around you?

PRAYER

Dear Lord, thank You for the gift of this new grandchild. May Your love surround this precious child and may our hearts be filled with joy as we watch them grow.

New life brings renewed promise and a fresh perspective on love.

TRUSTING GOD WITH OUR HOPES

"Yes, my soul, find rest in God; my hope comes from Him. Truly He is my rock and my salvation; He is my fortress, I will not be shaken." **Psalm 62:5-6**

DEVOTIONAL

As we release our dreams and desires into His hands, we open ourselves to the abundance of His grace and the joy of His unexpected blessings.

What hopes do you hold in your heart that you can trust God with today?

PRAYER

Dear Lord, as I lay my hopes before You, help me to trust in Your perfect timing and wisdom. Fill my heart with peace and assurance as I lean into Your promises.

Trusting God transforms our hopes into a beautiful tapestry of His grace.

NEW LIFE IN CHRIST

"A garment of praise instead of a spirit of despair."
Isaiah 61:3

DEVOTIONAL

Just as the earth awakens to new life each spring, may we also open our hearts to the renewal that Christ offers, trusting in His promise to bring beauty from our struggles.

What new beginnings is God inviting you to embrace this spring, and how can you nurture that new life in your heart?

PRAYER

Dear Lord, thank You for the gift of new life in Christ. Help me to open my heart to the beauty of spring, embracing the fresh starts You offer every day. Amen.

In Christ, every spring carries the promise of renewal and hope.

MARCH 2

THE JOY OF GARDENING

"They are like trees planted by streams of water, which yield their fruit in season and their leaves do not wither." **Psalm 1:3**

DEVOTIONAL

In nurturing our gardens, we find echoes of the love we've cultivated in our families, reminding us that growth often begins with tender care and patience.

What joys have you discovered in your garden that reflect the love and nourishment you give to your family? How does tending to your plants bring peace to your heart?

PRAYER

Dear Lord, thank You for the beauty and tranquility found in nature. May my days spent in the garden be filled with Your presence and love, reminding me of the joy You bring to my life.

Every flower you nurture echoes the love you've sown in your family.

PRAYING FOR OUR CHURCH FAMILY

"For where two or three gather in my name, there am I with them."
Matthew 18:20

DEVOTIONAL

Let us remember that our prayers for one another are the threads that keep our church family connected and strong.

What comes to your heart when you think about the needs of your church family? Who in your community might be longing for your prayers today?

PRAYER

Dear Lord, thank You for blessing us with a loving church family. Please strengthen our bonds and draw us closer together as we lift each other up in prayer.

In nurturing our church family through prayer,
we weave a tapestry of love that envelops us all.

THE BLESSING OF A DAUGHTER

"Her children rise up and call her blessed; her husband also,
and he praises her." Proverbs 31:28

DEVOTIONAL

The joy of having a daughter is not just in the moments shared but in the legacy of love that blossoms through her relationships with others.

What does it mean to you to be a grandmother to a daughter? How have your experiences shaped your relationship with her?

PRAYER

Dear Lord, thank you for the precious gift of our daughters. Help us to cherish our memories and continue to nurture our bond with love and grace.

A daughter's laughter is a melody that resonates in a grandmother's heart.

MARCH 5

THE GIFT OF A SON

"For God so loved the world that He gave His one and only Son, that whoever believes in Him shall not perish but have eternal life." John 3:16

DEVOTIONAL

Cherish the gift of family, for each child and grandchild is a reflection of the love we've been given and a promise for the future.

What memories do you hold dear about your son, and how have they enriched your understanding of love and grace in your life?

PRAYER

Dear Lord, thank You for the precious gift of family, especially for the joy that a son brings into our lives. Help us to cherish these moments and to love unconditionally, reflecting Your grace.

A son is not just a blessing; he is a reminder of the love that binds generations together.

MARCH 6

THE IMPORTANCE OF PATIENCE

"Let perseverance finish its work so that you may be mature and complete, not lacking anything." James 1:4

DEVOTIONAL

In our journey, patience teaches us that beautiful fruits emerge in their own time, bringing rewards we often cannot see at first.

What does patience look like in your daily life, and how can you cultivate it in your relationships with family and friends?

PRAYER

Dear Lord, thank You for the gift of time and for the lessons it brings. Help me to embrace each moment with grace and patience as I navigate the blessings and challenges of life.

Patience is the gentle strength that allows love to blossom in its own time.

THE POWER OF A THANKFUL HEART

"In everything give thanks; for this is the will of God in Christ Jesus concerning you." 1 Thessalonians 5:18

DEVOTIONAL

Through the simple act of thankfulness, we can transform life's little challenges into opportunities for joy and love.

What are three things you can be thankful for today, and how have they impacted your heart and spirit? Consider how gratitude has shaped your perspective in this season of life.

PRAYER

Dear God, thank you for the gift of each new day. Help me to see the blessings in my life and cultivate a heart overflowing with gratitude.

A thankful heart transforms ordinary days into extraordinary blessings.

CELEBRATING WOMEN

"But I will hope continually and will praise you yet more and more." Psalm 71:14

DEVOTIONAL

In every friendship and support we offer one another, we create a tapestry of love that celebrates our shared journey.

What women have inspired you in your life, and how can you honor their contributions in your own journey today? Think about the legacies they've left and how they continue to shape who you are.

PRAYER

Dear God, thank You for the incredible women who have paved the way for us. Help us to celebrate their strength and wisdom as we reflect on their impact in our lives and communities. May we also encourage and uplift the women around us today.

Every woman is a story, a legacy of strength, resilience, and love.

MARCH 9

THE BLESSING OF A CLOSE FRIEND

"Therefore encourage one another and build each other up, just as in fact you are doing. 1 Thessalonians 5:11

DEVOTIONAL

The blessing of a close friend reminds us that love and encouragement can brighten even the cloudiest of days.

What does your close friend mean to you, and how have they enriched your life through shared experiences and heartfelt conversations?

PRAYER

Dear Lord, thank you for the precious gift of friendship. Please nurture and strengthen the bonds we share, reminding us daily of the love and joy that true friends bring.

Friendship is a treasure that shines brightest
in life's gentle moments and steadfast storms.

MARCH 10

THE GIFT OF MUSIC

"Make a joyful noise unto the Lord, all ye lands. Serve the Lord with gladness: come before His presence with singing." Psalm 100:1

DEVOTIONAL

Music is a beautiful gift that transcends time, allowing us to share love and joy, no matter our age.

What song comes to your mind when you think about moments of joy in your life, and how does that music resonate with your heart today?

PRAYER

Dear Lord, thank you for the gift of music that fills our lives with joy and connection. May each note remind us of your love and grace as we bask in the melodies of our memories.

Music is the silent language of the heart,
speaking truths that words often cannot.

PRAYING FOR OUR COMMUNITY

"And let us consider how we may spur one another on toward love and good deeds, not giving up meeting together, as some are in the habit of doing, but encouraging one another—and all the more as you see the Day approaching." **Hebrews 10:24-25**

DEVOTIONAL

Sometimes, all it takes to bring a community together is the gentle nudge of prayer and the willingness to act with love.

What are some specific needs within your community that you feel moved to pray for today? How might your prayers impact those around you?

PRAYER

Dear God, thank you for our beautiful community filled with unique souls. Please guide us to be a source of love and support for one another, helping us lift up those who may be struggling.

Your prayers can be the light that guides someone through their darkest hour.

MARCH 12

THE JOY OF SPRING CLEANING

"Create in me a clean heart, O God, and renew a right spirit within me." **Psalm 51:10**

DEVOTIONAL

Just as we clear the clutter from our homes, let us also make space in our hearts for new blessings and fresh experiences.

What hidden treasures or memories do you uncover when you take the time to tidy up your space?

PRAYER

Dear Lord, thank you for the gift of a new season and the opportunity for renewal. As we clear away the clutter in our homes, help us to also embrace the changes in our hearts. May your joy fill our spirits as we refresh our surroundings.

Just as the flowers bloom with the season, so too can our hearts blossom with joy through the act of letting go.

MARCH 13

THE BEAUTY OF GOD'S CREATION

"O Lord, how manifold are Your works! In wisdom, You have made them all; the earth is full of Your creatures. There is the sea, vast and spacious, teeming with creatures beyond number—living things both large and small." Psalm 104:24-25

DEVOTIONAL

Every day holds the opportunity to witness the beauty of God's creation; let it inspire your heart and remind you of His infinite love.

What special moment in nature have you recently experienced that reminded you of God's loving presence? How did it make you feel to witness His handiwork?

PRAYER

Dear Lord, thank you for the beauty that surrounds us each day. Help us to see and appreciate your creation in all its forms, from the smallest flower to the vast sky above. Amen.

In the gentle whisper of the breeze, we hear the heart of our Creator.

MARCH 14

THE IMPORTANCE OF REST

"He makes me lie down in green pastures. He leads me beside still waters." Psalm 23:2

DEVOTIONAL

Sometimes, a little pause in our busy lives can refresh both our spirits and our hearts, reminding us that rest is a vital part of our journey.

What does rest mean to you in this season of life, and how might you embrace it more intentionally in your daily routine?

PRAYER

Dear Lord, thank You for the gift of rest and quiet moments. Help me to prioritize my need for peace and refreshment, so I may embrace each day with joy and strength. Amen.

Rest is not a luxury; it is a meeting place with our Creator.

THE BLESSING OF A GRANDSON

"Impress them on your children. Talk about them when you sit at home and when you walk along the road, when you lie down and when you get up." **Deuteronomy 6:7**

DEVOTIONAL
Cherish each moment with your grandson, for in his innocence, there lies a profound connection to your legacy of love and faith.

What are the special moments you cherish with your grandson that remind you of the joy he brings into your life? How can you nurture those moments even more?

PRAYER
Dear Lord, thank You for the gift of my grandson. May our bond grow stronger and may I always see the beauty in our shared moments.

Each laugh, each hug, and each story shared are treasures woven into the fabric of our hearts.

THE GIFT OF A GRANDDAUGHTER

"Only be careful, and watch yourselves closely so that you do not forget the things your eyes have seen or let them fade from your heart as long as you live. Teach them to your children and to their children after them." **Deuteronomy 4:9**

DEVOTIONAL
Every moment spent with your granddaughter is a precious treasure that not only enriches her life but also deepens your legacy and joy.

What special moments have you shared with your granddaughter that fill your heart with joy?

PRAYER
Dear God, thank you for the precious gift of granddaughters. May our bonds deepen and our shared memories grow sweeter with each passing day.

Every moment spent with a granddaughter is a treasure, a thread woven into the fabric of your heart.

MARCH 17

CELEBRATING FAMILY ROOTS

"A good man leaves an inheritance to his children's children."
Proverbs 13:22

DEVOTIONAL

The greatest gift we can give our grandchildren is the legacy of our stories and the values that have shaped our lives.

What are the cherished stories and traditions from your family that you can share with your grandchildren today? How can these lessons help strengthen your family's bonds in the future?

PRAYER

Dear Lord, thank You for the gift of family and the rich tapestry of our heritage. May we honor and celebrate our roots, sharing love and wisdom with those who come after us.

Roots nourish us, and the stories we pass down
are the branches that keep our family tree flourishing.

MARCH 18

THE POWER OF PRAYER

"And whatever you ask in prayer, you will receive, if you have faith."
Matthew 21:22

DEVOTIONAL

Remember, every prayer, no matter how small, carries the strength of love and intention, forging a bond between you and your loved ones that nothing can break.

What moments in your life have shown you the importance of turning to prayer? How has prayer shaped your relationship with God and those around you?

PRAYER

Dear Lord, thank you for the gift of prayer. Help me to remember that in every moment, whether joyful or challenging, I can always turn to you for guidance and comfort.

Prayer is the bridge that connects our hearts to the Father's presence.

RENEWAL

"I will open rivers on the bare heights, and fountains in the midst of the valleys; I will make the wilderness a pool of water, and the dry land springs of water." Isaiah 41:18

DEVOTIONAL

Sometimes, renewal comes from nurturing old dreams while embracing new possibilities.

"What does renewal mean to you, and how can you embrace this season of spring in your own life?

PRAYER

Dear Lord, thank you for the beauty of spring and the promise of renewal it brings. May we open our hearts to new beginnings and be filled with your love and hope as we step into this season.

Just as flowers bloom after the frost,
our hearts can also blossom in times of change.

"

THE BLESSING OF FAMILY TRADITIONS

"And these words that I command you today shall be on your heart. You shall teach them diligently to your children and shall talk of them when you sit in your house, and when you walk by the way, and when you lie down, and when you rise." Deuteronomy 6:6-7

DEVOTIONAL

Grandchildren may forget the specifics of our stories, but they will always remember the warmth of our traditions and the love that surrounded them.

What family traditions bring you the most joy and connection? How do they reflect your love for your family and your hopes for future generations?

PRAYER

Dear Lord, thank You for the gift of family and the traditions that bind us together. Help us to cherish these moments and pass down our love and wisdom to those who come after us.

Traditions are the threads that weave the fabric of our family stories.

THE JOY OF LEARNING NEW THINGS

"The righteous will flourish like a palm tree, they will grow like a cedar of Lebanon; planted in the house of the Lord, they will flourish in the courts of our God. They will still bear fruit in old age, they will stay fresh and green." Psalm 92:12-14

DEVOTIONAL

Life is a beautiful journey of continuous learning, and embracing new experiences can bring fresh joy and connection, no matter your age.

What new skill or hobby have you been curious about lately, and how might exploring it bring you joy and connection with others?

PRAYER

Dear Lord, thank You for the gift of curiosity and the joy that comes with learning. Help me to embrace new opportunities with an open heart and a willing spirit.

Learning is a lifelong journey, and each new experience can weave beautiful threads into the tapestry of our lives.

THE GIFT OF HOSPITALITY

"Share with the Lord's people who are in need. Practice hospitality." Romans 12:13

DEVOTIONAL

A warm invitation can turn a stranger into a friend and make the simplest moments unforgettable.

What memories do you cherish of gathering friends and family around your table, and how can you create more moments like those in the days to come?

PRAYER

Dear Lord, thank you for the gift of community and the warmth of shared meals. Help me to open my home and my heart to others, creating a space filled with love and joy.

Hospitality is not just about food;
it's about making others feel at home in your heart.

PRAYING FOR OUR NATION

"Also, seek the peace and prosperity of the city to which I have carried you into exile. Pray to the Lord for it, because if it prospers, you too will prosper." Jeremiah 29:7

DEVOTIONAL

Let us remember, dear sisters, that our prayers hold the power to shape the future lives of our loved ones and our nation, so let us lift our voices in faith and love.

What are the specific concerns you carry for your nation, and how might your prayers influence those around you? Consider how your heart feels in this moment as you bring these thoughts to God.

PRAYER

Dear Lord, we come to You with heavy hearts for our nation. Guide our leaders and our people towards understanding, kindness, and unity. May our prayers be a balm for the wounds around us.

Prayer is the whisper of hope that can change the course of history.

THE BLESSING OF A LOVING HEART

"We love because he first loved us."
1 John 4:19

DEVOTIONAL

When we open our hearts to love freely, we create a cherished legacy that continues to bless generations.

What does it mean to you to have a loving heart, and how can you express that love in your daily interactions with family and friends?

PRAYER

Dear God, thank you for the gift of love in our hearts. Help us to share that love freely, nurturing those around us with kindness and compassion.

A loving heart not only transforms the lives of others
but enriches our own journey.

MARCH 25

THE IMPORTANCE OF FAITHFULNESS

"Therefore, my dear brothers and sisters, stand firm. Let nothing move you. Always give yourselves fully to the work of the Lord, because you know that your labor in the Lord is not in vain." **1 Corinthians 15:58**

DEVOTIONAL

Faithfulness, like a well-tended garden, requires patience and dedication, but the beauty it brings will bless not only you but generations to come.

What does faithfulness mean to you, and how has it shaped your relationships and experiences over the years?

PRAYER

Dear Lord, thank You for the gift of faithfulness in our lives. Help us to embrace and embody this quality, nurturing the bonds we have with family, friends, and You. May Your unwavering love inspire our hearts each day.

Faithfulness is the quiet strength that binds hearts together and nurtures a legacy of love.

MARCH 26

THE GIFT OF A LOVING PET

"Your righteousness is like the mighty mountains, your justice like the great deep. You, Lord, preserve both people and animals." **Psalm 36:6**

DEVOTIONAL

Cherish the simple joys that a loving pet brings into your life, as their unwavering companionship reflects the love of God in our everyday moments.

What joy does your furry friend bring to your life, and how have they taught you about love and companionship?

PRAYER

Dear Lord, thank You for the gift of our beloved pets. May we always cherish the unconditional love they bring into our lives. Help us to reflect Your love through the care we give them.

The heart grows warmer with every wag of a tail and every gentle purr.

THE JOY OF SHARING STORIES

"But as for you, speak the things which are proper for sound doctrine."
Titus 2:1

DEVOTIONAL

Every story you share holds the power to connect generations, bridging the past and the present with love and laughter.

What story has most shaped your life, and how can sharing it bring joy to others today?

PRAYER

Dear Lord, thank You for the gift of memories and the stories that bind us together. Help me to share my experiences with love and wisdom, bringing joy and lessons to those who listen.

Every story shared is a bridge built between generations.

MARCH 28

THE BLESSING OF A STRONG MARRIAGE

"A wife of noble character who can find? She is worth far more than rubies. Her husband has full confidence in her and lacks nothing of value."
Proverbs 31:10-11

DEVOTIONAL

A strong marriage is a beautiful example of enduring love that nourishes not only the couple but also the generations that follow.

What are some of the ways your strong marriage has shaped your life and the lives of those around you? Reflect on the moments that have brought you joy and deep connection.

PRAYER

Dear Lord, thank you for the gift of love that we share in our marriages. Help us to appreciate and nurture these bonds daily and to carry that love into the lives of our families.

Love is a lifelong journey – the roots that nourish our family tree.

MARCH 29

THE POWER OF HOPE

"May the God of hope fill you with all joy and peace as you trust in Him."
Romans 15:13

DEVOTIONAL

Hope clings to the heart and can transform even the most somber days
into a tapestry of love and connection.

*What brings you hope in your daily life, and how can you nurture that hope in
times of difficulty?*

PRAYER

Dear God, thank You for the gift of hope that anchors our souls. May we
feel Your presence in our hearts and find comfort in the promises You
have for us each day. Amen.

Hope lights the path even in the darkest moments,
guiding us toward the beauty of tomorrow.

MARCH 30

PREPARING FOR EASTER

"He is not here; for He has risen, as He said.
Come, see the place where He lay." **Matthew 28:6**

DEVOTIONAL

Let the spirit of renewal that comes with Easter inspire you to share love,
hope, and faith with your family, creating a legacy of joy that will bloom
for generations to come.

*What does Easter mean to you personally, and how can you prepare your heart and
home to embrace its joy this year?*

PRAYER

Dear Lord, as Easter approaches, help us to reflect on your love and grace.
Fill our hearts with joy and anticipation for the celebration of new life
through your resurrection.

Preparing for Easter is like nurturing a garden; the more care
and love we invest, the more beautiful the blooms we will see.

WELCOMING JESUS

"The crowds that went ahead of him and those that followed shouted, 'Hosanna to the Son of David!' 'Blessed is he who comes in the name of the Lord!' 'Hosanna in the highest heaven!'"
Matthew 21:9

DEVOTIONAL

We learn that welcoming others, much like welcoming Jesus into our hearts, creates bonds of love and joy that fill our lives with meaning.

What does it mean for you to welcome Jesus into your everyday life this Palm Sunday? How can you extend that same welcome to those around you?

PRAYER

Dear Lord, thank You for the gift of Your Son and the joy He brings into our lives. Help us to open our hearts wide and embrace Him as we prepare for this special day. Let our homes be filled with warmth and love, just as we welcome You in.

Welcoming Jesus is not just a gesture; it's a heartfelt invitation to let Him walk alongside us in our journey.

THE JOY OF LAUGHTER

"Our mouths were filled with laughter, our tongues with songs of joy."
Psalm 126:2

DEVOTIONAL

In the tapestry of life, laughter is one of the most vibrant colors that remind us to enjoy every moment and cherish our loved ones.

What brings you joy and laughter in your life right now? How can you cultivate more moments of light-heartedness with those you love?

PRAYER

Dear Lord, thank you for the gift of laughter and the joy it brings to our hearts. Help us to find humor in life's little moments and share that laughter with those around us.

Laughter is a gentle reminder that joy exists
even in the simplest of moments.

THE BLESSING OF A HUMBLE HEART

"For everyone who exalts himself will be humbled, but the one who humbles himself will be exalted." **Luke 18:14**

DEVOTIONAL

A humble heart opens the door to truly meaningful connections with others, no matter the struggles we face.

What does having a humble heart mean to you in your daily life, and how can you cultivate this quality in your interactions with family and friends?

PRAYER

Dear Lord, thank you for the gift of humility and the beauty it brings into our lives. Help us to embrace a humble heart, showing kindness and love in all that we do. Guide us in being a light to those around us.

A humble heart opens the door to countless blessings.

PRAYING FOR OUR SCHOOLS

"All your children shall be taught by the Lord, and great shall be the peace of your children." Isaiah 54:13

DEVOTIONAL

We may not walk the halls of schools anymore, but our prayers can still pave the way for the safety, guidance, and growth of those who do.

What concerns or hopes do you have for the children and educators in your local schools?

PRAYER

Dear Lord, we lift up our schools to You, asking for Your guidance and protection over every child and teacher. May Your love and wisdom fill those hallways and classrooms, bringing peace and understanding.

Prayer is the most powerful tool we have
to shape the future of our children.

THE GIFT OF SPRING RAIN

"...for as the rain comes down, and the snow from heaven, and do not return there, but water the earth, and make it bring forth and bud, that it may give seed to the sower and bread to the eater." Isaiah 55:10

DEVOTIONAL

Just as spring rain rejuvenates the earth, our love and prayers can nurture our families, helping them to grow and flourish in their own seasons of life.

What memories do you hold dear that remind you of spring's refreshing rains, and how have these moments shaped your view of renewal in your life?

PRAYER

Dear Father, thank you for the gift of spring rains that nourish our world and our spirits. Help us to embrace the refreshing moments in our lives, trusting in Your perfect timing for new beginnings.

Just as the spring rain brings forth new life,
so too can our hearts blossom with hope and joy.

THE POWER OF A GENTLE TOUCH

"Let your gentleness be evident to all. The Lord is near."
Philippians 4:5

DEVOTIONAL

A gentle touch can heal wounds that words cannot reach and offers comfort when the world feels heavy.

What gentle touches have you shared with those in your life, and how might you use them to uplift someone today?

PRAYER

Dear Lord, help me to embrace the power of my gentle touch—whether it be through a soft hug, a kind word, or a loving gesture. May my hands be instruments of Your love in the lives of those around me.

In a world that often rushes, your gentle touch can be the stillness someone needs.

THE BEAUTY OF NEW GROWTH

"Those who are planted in the house of the Lord shall flourish in the courts of our God. They shall still bear fruit in old age; they shall be fresh and flourishing." Psalm 92:13-14

DEVOTIONAL

No matter our age, we are always capable of flowering beautifully in God's garden.

What new beginnings are sprouting in your life right now? How can you nurture these moments of growth and allow them to flourish?

PRAYER

Dear God, thank You for the gift of new life and fresh starts. Please open our hearts to recognize the beauty of growth in our lives, no matter our age.

Just as a flower blooms anew each spring, so too can our spirits awaken with fresh hope and joy.

THE BLESSING OF A FAMILY RECIPE

"Do not forget to entertain strangers, for by so doing some have unwittingly entertained angels." **Hebrews 13:2**

DEVOTIONAL

The most cherished moments in life often bloom around the table where family recipes are shared, becoming the heart of our stories and traditions.

What is a family recipe that brings back cherished memories for you, and how can you share its warmth with your loved ones today?

PRAYER

Dear Lord, thank You for the gift of family and the recipes that bind us together. May our kitchens be filled with love as we create and share these precious traditions.

Recipes are love made visible, connecting generations through flavors and stories.

THE GIFT OF A QUIET MORNING

"But when you pray, go into your room, close the door and pray to your Father, who is unseen. Then your Father, who sees what is done in secret, will reward you." **Matthew 6:6**

DEVOTIONAL

In a world that often rushes by, cherishing the peace of a quiet morning allows us to reconnect with our hearts and the blessings around us.

What does a quiet morning mean to you, and how can you embrace those moments to connect more deeply with yourself and God?

PRAYER

Dear Lord, thank You for the gift of each new day and the stillness that mornings bring. May I find peace and joy as I sit quietly in Your presence, welcoming all that You wish to share with me.

In the stillness of the morning, we discover the whispers of our hearts and the gentle nudges of grace.

PRAYING FOR OUR PASTORS

"I thank my God every time I remember you. In all my prayers for all of you, I always pray with joy because of your partnership in the gospel from the first day until now." **Philippians 1:3-5**

DEVOTIONAL

Every prayer can provide strength and encouragement to our pastors, reminding them they are not alone in their journey.

"What specific qualities do you appreciate in your pastor, and how can you pray for those traits to flourish even more in their life and ministry?

PRAYER

Dear Lord, bless our pastors with strength and wisdom as they guide us. May they feel your love surrounding them and find comfort in your presence daily.

When we pray for our leaders, we weave a tapestry of support that uplifts not only them but our whole community.

THE JOY OF EASTER PREPARATIONS

"So with you: Now is your time of grief, but I will see you again and you will rejoice, and no one will take away your joy." **John 16:22**

DEVOTIONAL

In the busy preparations of Easter, remember to weave joy into the moments spent with family, for it is in these joyful acts where our faith flourishes.

What small yet meaningful traditions can you embrace this Easter to fill your heart with joy and create lasting memories with your family?

PRAYER

Heavenly Father, thank You for the gift of renewal that Easter brings. Help me to prepare my heart and home in joyful anticipation of this special season, sharing love and warmth with those around me.

Preparation transforms our hearts, making room for the joy of resurrection and new beginnings.

THE BLESSING OF A FAMILY HEIRLOOM

"If you then, being evil, know how to give good gifts to your children, how much more will your Father who is in heaven give good things to those who ask Him?" Matthew 7:11

DEVOTIONAL

Every piece of history we share with our loved ones holds the power to enrich their lives and strengthen familial bonds.

What family heirloom do you cherish the most, and how has it shaped your understanding of love and legacy within your family?

PRAYER

Dear God, thank you for the treasures of our families that connect us across generations. Help us to honor our heritage and pass on love and wisdom to those who will follow.

Each heirloom carries a story, weaving together
the hearts of generations past and present.

THE GIFT OF A LISTENING EAR

"Let every man be swift to hear, slow to speak, and slow to wrath."
James 1:19

DEVOTIONAL

Listening is a profound act of love that can heal hearts and strengthen bonds.

What are some moments in your life when you felt heard and valued, and how can you offer that same gift to those around you?

PRAYER

Dear Lord, thank you for the gift of listening and for those who take the time to hear our hearts. Help me to offer my ears and my heart to others, creating a space where they feel cherished and understood.

The beauty of a listening ear is that it can
heal wounds we didn't even know we carried.

APRIL 13

THE POWER OF A MOTHER'S PRAYER

"Surely the arm of the Lord is not too short to save,
nor his ear too dull to hear." Isaiah 59:1

DEVOTIONAL

Your prayers, Grandma, are powerful and hold the potential to change
lives, even when the needs seem overwhelming.

*What is the most cherished prayer you remember your mother offering on your
behalf, and how does it continue to shape your life today?*

PRAYER

Dear Lord, thank You for the gift of prayer and the love that flows through
it. May I always feel the warmth of Your presence in my life and the lives of
my children and grandchildren. Help me to lift them up in prayer daily.

Each prayer I whisper carries the weight of love and faith.

APRIL 14

THE BLESSING OF A FAMILY PHOTO

"For I will pour water on the thirsty land, and streams on the dry ground; I
will pour out My Spirit on your offspring, and My blessing on your
descendants." Isaiah 44:3

DEVOTIONAL

Every time you gather your family for a photo, remember that it's not just
a picture, but a beautiful testimony of love that bridges generations.

*What emotions stir within you when you look at a family photo? How do the faces
in that picture remind you of the love and memories you've cultivated over the
years?*

PRAYER

Dear Lord, thank You for the gift of family and the memories we hold
dear. May we cherish each moment captured in our hearts and
photographs, and may they serve as a reminder of Your blessings in our
lives.

Every picture tells a story of love and legacy.

TRUSTING GOD WITH FINANCES

"Keep your lives free from the love of money and be content with what you have, because God has said, 'Never will I leave you; never will I forsake you.'" **Hebrews 13:5**

DEVOTIONAL

Even when our financial situations seem dire, trusting God opens our hearts to the rich blessings of His provision.

What does trusting God with your finances look like for you in this season of life, and how can you embrace His provision amid your worries?

PRAYER

Dear Heavenly Father, thank You for being our ultimate provider. Help us to place our trust in You, even when financial strains arise, knowing that You see our needs and care for us deeply.

God's faithfulness is our anchor in the storm of uncertainty.

APRIL 16

THE GIFT OF A SPRING WALK

"For everything there is a season,
and a time for every matter under heaven." **Ecclesiastes 3:1**

DEVOTIONAL

Sometimes, the simple act of stepping outside into the warmth of the sun can uncover delightful moments waiting to be shared.

What joys do you discover in nature during your spring walks, and how do they remind you of the beauty of God's creations in your own life?

PRAYER

Dear Lord, thank you for the beauty of spring and the gentle reminders of your love found in every blossom and gentle breeze. Help me to appreciate each moment I have to connect with nature and your presence.

Every step you take is a step towards gratitude
and peace in God's creation.

APRIL 17

THE JOY OF A CHILD'S LAUGHTER

"A cheerful heart brings a smile to your face; a sad heart makes it hard to get through the day." **Proverbs 15:13**

DEVOTIONAL

Never underestimate the power of laughter to brighten your day and create memories that last a lifetime.

What moments have you shared with your grandchildren that made you laugh the hardest? How does their laughter fill your heart with joy?

PRAYER

Dear Lord, thank you for the gift of laughter and the joy it brings to our lives. Help us to cherish the moments of joy and silliness we share with our grandchildren, and to always embrace the love that fills the air during those precious times.

Laughter is the music of the heart,
a symphony that resonates with the purest of joys.

APRIL 18

THE BLESSING OF A FAMILY GATHERING

"Behold, how good and pleasant it is when brothers dwell in unity!"
Psalm 133:1

DEVOTIONAL

Family gatherings are not just about food and festivities; they are a cherished time to nurture relationships and create memories that endure through the years.

What cherished memories do you hold from family gatherings that have filled your heart with joy?

PRAYER

Dear Lord, thank You for the gift of family and the beautiful moments we share. May our gatherings be filled with love, laughter, and connection, binding our hearts even closer together.

Every family gathering is a stitch in the tapestry of our lives, creating patterns of love and connection that last through generations.

THE GIFT OF A NEW FRIEND

"My help comes from the Lord, the Maker of heaven and earth."
Psalm 121:2

DEVOTIONAL

Embrace every opportunity for new friendships, for they are often a gift from God, bringing warmth and joy in unexpected seasons of life.

What does friendship mean to you in this season of life, and how can you open your heart to new connections?

PRAYER

Dear Lord, thank You for the gift of friendship. Help me to embrace new relationships with an open heart and to cherish the wisdom that comes from sharing life with others. Amen.

Every new friend is a treasure waiting to be discovered.

THE POWER OF RESURRECTION HOPE

"Blessed be the God and Father of our Lord Jesus Christ, who according to His great mercy has caused us to be born again to a living hope through the resurrection of Jesus Christ from the dead." **1 Peter 1:3**

DEVOTIONAL

Just like Mabel, we all weather seasons of sorrow, but the promise of resurrection hope reminds us that love is eternal and our connections are never truly lost.

What does the idea of resurrection hope mean to you in this season of life? How can you carry this hope into your daily interactions with family and friends?

PRAYER

Dear Lord, thank You for the promise of resurrection and renewal in our lives. Help me to embrace this hope daily and share its warmth with those I love. May I be a beacon of Your light and life.

With every ending, God prepares
a new beginning filled with hope and possibility.

APRIL 21

HE IS RISEN!

"I am the resurrection and the life. He who believes in me will live, even though he dies; and whoever lives and believes in me will never die."
John 11:25-26

DEVOTIONAL

This Easter, let the hope of resurrection fill your heart with joy, reminding you that love is everlasting.

What does the resurrection of Jesus mean for you in this season of your life, and how can you share that hope with those around you?

PRAYER

Dear Lord, thank You for the gift of Your Son and the joy of His resurrection. Help us to carry this hope in our hearts today, sharing it with family and friends in meaningful ways.

He is risen not just to offer us eternal life
but to fill our days with purpose and joy.

APRIL 22

CARING FOR GOD'S CREATION

"You will go out in joy and be led forth in peace; the mountains and hills will burst into song before you, and all the trees of the field will clap their hands." Isaiah 55:12

DEVOTIONAL

Every small act of caring for the earth brings us closer to God and to the beauty of community, building a legacy of stewardship for the generations to come.

What do you cherish most about the beauty of nature, and how can you share that love with your family and community?

PRAYER

Dear Creator, thank you for the gift of your creation that surrounds us every day. Help us to cherish and protect the earth, nurturing it for future generations to enjoy. Amen.

Every flower, every tree, is a reminder of God's
boundless love and artistry.

THE BLESSING OF A FAMILY TRADITION

"This is my commandment, that you love one another as I have loved you."
John 15:12

DEVOTIONAL

Family traditions, no matter how small, weave a tapestry of love and connection that lasts across generations.

What family traditions have brought you joy over the years, and how can you pass those cherished moments to the next generation?

PRAYER

Dear Lord, thank you for the gift of family and the traditions that bind us together. Help me to cherish and share the blessings of our past, nurturing the love that flows in our family.

Traditions are the threads that weave our family stories
into a beautiful tapestry of love and memory.

THE GIFT OF A HANDWRITTEN NOTE

"The righteous who walks in his integrity—blessed are his children after him." **Proverbs 20:7**

DEVOTIONAL

Let your words flow freely in handwritten notes, for they are gifts of love that create lasting memories and offer comfort to those you cherish.

What memory comes to mind when you think of a handwritten note you've received? How did it make you feel, and how might you replicate that joy for someone in your life today?

PRAYER

Dear God, thank You for the gift of words and the hearts they touch. Help me to share my love and encouragement through handwritten notes, reminding others they are cherished.

A simple note can become a treasure,
warming hearts and strengthening bonds.

THE JOY OF SPRING FLOWERS

"The wilderness and the solitary place shall be glad for them; and the desert shall rejoice, and blossom as the rose. It shall blossom abundantly..."
Isaiah 35:1-2a

DEVOTIONAL

Just as spring flowers bloom after a time of waiting, we too can nurture the seeds of joy in our lives, trusting that there is a season for everything.

What are your favorite memories associated with spring flowers, and how can you cultivate joy in your life this season?

PRAYER

Dear Lord, thank You for the beauty of spring and the joy it brings to our hearts. Help us to see and celebrate the small wonders around us, reminding us of Your love and grace. Amen.

Just as flowers bloom in their time,
so too do our lives blossom with the love we share.

THE BLESSING OF A FAMILY VACATION

"Your wife will be like a fruitful vine within your house; your children will be like olive shoots around your table." **Psalm 128:3**

DEVOTIONAL

Let each family vacation be a reminder that the greatest treasures aren't found in material things, but in the love and laughter shared around the table.

What memories do you cherish most from family vacations, and how can you create new ones this year?

PRAYER

Dear Lord, thank you for the gift of family and the joy of shared experiences. May our time together bring us closer and fill our hearts with laughter and love.

Family vacations are the threads that weave
together the fabric of our memories.

THE GIFT OF A LOVING SIBLING

"The Lord will guide you always; He will satisfy your needs in a sun-scorched land and will strengthen your frame. You will be like a well-watered garden, like a spring whose waters never fail." Isaiah 58:11

DEVOTIONAL

Cherish the beauty of sibling love, for it is a precious treasure that can bring warmth and comfort in every season of life.

What are some cherished memories you have with your sibling that remind you of the love you share?

PRAYER

Dear Lord, thank you for the precious gift of family. May our hearts be forever grateful for the love and support of our siblings as we journey through life together.

Siblings are the threads that weave the
fabric of our lives with love and laughter.

THE POWER OF A GRATEFUL HEART

"Give thanks to the LORD, for he is good; his love endures forever."
Psalm 136:1

DEVOTIONAL

The more we recognize and express gratitude, the more joy fills our lives, making each day a little sweeter.

*What in your life today can you express gratitude for,
and how does it make you feel to acknowledge those blessings?*

PRAYER

Dear Lord, thank you for the gift of each new day. Help me to see the beauty in my life and to carry a heart full of gratitude in every moment.

A grateful heart is like a sunflower,
turning towards the light of God's love.

APRIL 29

THE BLESSING OF A FAMILY PET

"A righteous man regards the life of his animal, but the tender mercies of the wicked are cruel." **Proverbs 12:10**

DEVOTIONAL

Our pets teach us unconditional love and patience, reminding us that the bonds we share with them can illuminate even the darkest days.

What special moments have you shared with your beloved pet that bring joy to your heart?

PRAYER

Dear Lord, thank You for the comfort and companionship our pets bring into our lives. Help us to cherish the love and joy they offer us daily. May we always see the blessing they are in our family.

In the gentle purring of a cat or the playful wag of a dog, we find love in its purest form.

APRIL 30

THE GIFT OF A NEW SEASON

"I am confident of this, that he who began a good work in you will carry it on to completion until the day of Christ Jesus." **Philippians 1:6**

DEVOTIONAL

Embrace each new season as a beautiful opportunity to grow and bloom in ways you never imagined possible.

What new opportunities or joys do you feel God is inviting you to explore in this season of your life?

PRAYER

Dear Lord, thank You for the gift of new seasons in our lives. Help us to embrace the changes with open hearts and to trust in Your loving plan.

Every season of life carries the promise of fresh beginnings.

MAY 1

SPREADING KINDNESS

"And let us not grow weary of doing good, for in due season we will reap, if we do not give up." Galatians 6:9

DEVOTIONAL
Spreading kindness, just like seeds in a garden, allows love to bloom unexpectedly in the hearts around us.

What acts of kindness have you witnessed or participated in recently, and how did they make you feel? Can you think of a way to spread a little more kindness in your community this May Day?

PRAYER
Dear Lord, thank you for the gift of love and kindness you show us each day. Help us to share that love and kindness with others, lighting up their lives as we walk through each moment together.

Kindness is the sunshine that warms the hearts of those around us.

MAY 2

THE BLESSING OF A MOTHER'S LOVE

"As a mother comforts her child, so will I comfort you; and you will be comforted over Jerusalem." Isaiah 66:13

DEVOTIONAL
A mother's love is an everlasting gift that nurtures our hearts and souls, creating a legacy of strength and affection for our families.

What moments in your life can you look back on and see the gentle touch of your mother's love guiding you? How has that love shaped the woman you are today?

PRAYER
Dear Lord, thank You for the gift of a mother's love that nurtures and strengthens us. Help us to carry that love forward in our families, shining Your light through our actions and words.

A mother's love is a tapestry woven with threads of grace, patience, and unending support.

MAY 3

THE GIFT OF A FAMILY GARDEN

"But the fruit of the Spirit is love, joy, peace, forbearance, kindness, goodness, faithfulness, gentleness and self-control. Against such things there is no law." Galatians 5:22-23

DEVOTIONAL

The family garden is more than just a place for flowers and vegetables; it is a living testament to the bonds we cultivate, reminding us that love and nurturing thrive in the simplest of acts.

What are the precious memories you have cultivated with your family in your garden, and how can you nurture those blossoms in the seasons to come?

PRAYER

Dear Lord, thank You for the gift of family and the beauty of our gardens. May we cherish every moment spent together, planting seeds of love and joy in our hearts.

Every flower in the garden tells a story, much like every grandchild carries a piece of our heart.

MAY 4

THE JOY OF WATCHING GRANDCHILDREN GROW

"The Lord your God is in your midst, a mighty one who will save; he will rejoice over you with gladness; he will quiet you by his love; he will exult over you with loud singing." Zephaniah 3:17

DEVOTIONAL

Every giggle, every fall, and every hug are reminders that watching our grandchildren grow is one of life's greatest gifts.

What are the moments you've cherished most as you've watched your grandchildren grow, and how have those memories shaped your heart?

PRAYER

Dear Lord, thank You for the gift of grandchildren, for the joy they bring into our lives. Help us to appreciate each precious moment and to create lasting memories together.

Each laugh, each achievement, and every small step they take is a thread woven into the tapestry of our hearts.

CELEBRATING DIVERSITY

"After this I looked, and there before me was a great multitude that no one could count, from every nation, tribe, people, and language, standing before the throne and before the Lamb." Revelation 7:9

DEVOTIONAL

Remember, each person you meet carries a unique story and a piece of the Creator's handiwork that adds to the beautiful tapestry of life.

What does celebrating diversity mean to you in your life and family? How can you embrace and share different cultures with your loved ones this Cinco de Mayo?

PRAYER

Dear Lord, thank you for the beautiful tapestry of cultures that enrich our lives. Help us to appreciate and celebrate the diversity around us, instilling joy and understanding in our families.

Embracing diversity allows us to weave richer stories in the fabric of our lives.

THE BLESSING OF A FAMILY LEGACY

"For I know that my Redeemer lives, and he will stand upon the earth at last." Job 19:25

DEVOTIONAL

The greatest gift you can pass down is not just material inheritance but the love and values that define your family legacy.

What stories or values from your own upbringing do you hope to pass down to future generations? How can you nurture those in your family today?

PRAYER

Dear Lord, thank you for the gift of family and the legacy we create through love. Help us to cherish our shared moments and instill in our loved ones the values that sustain us.

Family is the thread that weaves our lives into a beautiful tapestry of love and memories.

MAY 7

THE GIFT OF A FAMILY STORY

"But as for me and my house, we will serve the Lord."
Joshua 24:15

DEVOTIONAL

Cherishing our family stories keeps us connected through time, allowing us to share wisdom and love with those who come after us.

What stories from your family history bring you warmth and joy? How can you share them with younger generations to weave a tapestry of love and connection?

PRAYER

Dear Lord, thank you for the gift of family and the stories that bind us together. Help me to cherish these tales and share them with others, so that the love and wisdom of our past may continue to live on.

Every family story is a thread in the beautiful fabric of our lives, connecting us through time and love.

MAY 8

THE POWER OF A FAITHFUL LIFE

"They will still bear fruit in old age; they will stay fresh and green."
Psalm 92:14

DEVOTIONAL

A faithful life is like a garden tended with love; both can thrive beautifully, no matter the seasons of life.

What moments in your life have shown you the strength of your faith? How have those experiences shaped your heart and spirit?

PRAYER

Dear Lord, thank you for the journey of faith you have laid before me. Help me to nurture a heart that reflects your love and steadfastness every day.

Faithful living is not just about great moments;
it's in the quiet, everyday choices that our love for God shines.

THE BLESSING OF A FAMILY MEAL

"Therefore welcome one another as Christ has welcomed you, for the glory of God." Romans 15:7

DEVOTIONAL

In the beauty of a family meal, we welcome one another in love, creating a tapestry of connection that honors our God-given place within the family.

"What memories do you cherish most from family meals, and how can you invite those moments into your heart today?

PRAYER

Dear Lord, thank you for the gift of family and the joy that comes from gathering around the table. May our conversations be filled with love and laughter, and may each shared meal deepen our connections.

Every meal shared is a sacred moment, a thread weaving together the fabric of our family's story.

MAY 10

THE GIFT OF A MOTHER'S DAY CARD

"Likewise, teach the older women to be reverent in the way they live, not to be slanderers or addicted to much wine, but to teach what is good. Then they can urge the younger women to love their husbands and children." Titus 2:3-4

DEVOTIONAL

Always cherish the messages of love you've given and received, knowing that the gift of a card, however simple, carries with it a world of memories and gratitude.

What memories do you cherish when you think of cards you've received from your loved ones, and how do they make you feel connected to them, even when they are not nearby?

PRAYER

Dear Lord, thank You for the gift of love shared through small gestures like a Mother's Day card. May we always appreciate these tokens of affection and remember the warm feelings they bring into our lives.

A mother's love is a written word that never fades away.

HONORING GENERATIONS

"Her children rise up and call her blessed; her husband also,
and he praises her." **Proverbs 31:29**

DEVOTIONAL

Cherish the stories and lessons shared with you, for they are treasures that
enrich not just your life, but the lives of those who come after you.

*What are some cherished memories you hold of the mothers in your life, and how do
those experiences shape your role in your family today?*

PRAYER

Dear Lord, thank you for the gift of generations that have shaped us. Help
us to honor and celebrate the legacy of love passed down through our
families today.

In honoring our mothers, we weave the threads of love
that bind the generations together.

THE JOY OF BEING A GRANDMA

"The Lord has done great things for us, and we are filled with joy."
Psalm 126:3

DEVOTIONAL

In the heart of every grandmother lies the warmth of connection,
reminding us that even in life's simplest moments, love creates lasting
memories.

*What brings you the most joy when you think of your role as a grandmother? How
do those special moments with your grandchildren make your heart feel?*

PRAYER

Dear Lord, thank you for the gift of grandchildren that fill our hearts with
love. Help us to cherish every moment we share and to impart wisdom in
the simplest of ways. May our days be filled with laughter and lasting
memories.

Being a grandmother is an endless treasure chest
of love and memories just waiting to be opened.

THE BLESSING OF A FAMILY OUTING

"Let the little children come to me, and do not hinder them, for to such belongs the kingdom of God." Luke 18:16

DEVOTIONAL

Deeply cherished memories are often made in simple outings, where love is the main dish served alongside laughter and connection.

What fond memories do you treasure from past family outings, and how have those moments shaped your family's bonds today?

PRAYER

Dear Lord, thank you for the gift of family and the joy that comes from spending time together. May every outing become a cherished memory, filled with laughter and love.

Together, we weave the tapestry of our family, colored with love, laughter, and unforgettable moments.

MAY 14

THE GIFT OF A FAMILY PRAYER

"Before they call, I will answer; while they are still speaking, I will hear." Isaiah 65:24

DEVOTIONAL

In the quiet act of gathering together in prayer, we nurture a legacy of love and faith that spans generations.

What does the gift of family prayer mean to you, and how has it shaped the bonds you share with your loved ones? Consider the moments when you gathered together, seeking guidance and strength through prayer.

PRAYER

Dear Lord, thank You for the family we cherish and the moments we share in Your presence. Bless the time we spend in prayer, and may it strengthen our love and unity.

Prayer is the thread that binds the hearts of a family together.

THE POWER OF A GENTLE SPIRIT

"Let your beauty be hidden in your heart, the unfading beauty of a gentle and quiet spirit, which is of great worth in God's sight." 1 Peter 3:4

DEVOTIONAL

Remember, dear ones, it's often through our gentle spirits that we offer the deepest comfort and understanding to those we love.

What does it mean to you to embody a gentle spirit in your daily interactions with family and friends? How can you cultivate this quality further in your life?

PRAYER

Dear Lord, thank You for the gift of a gentle spirit. Help me to embrace kindness and patience in all my dealings, reflecting Your love in everything I say and do.

A gentle spirit is a silent strength that nurtures and uplifts those around us.

THE BLESSING OF A FAMILY CELEBRATION

"Let all that you do be done in love."
1 Corinthians 16:14

DEVOTIONAL

Family celebrations are the threads that weave our family's tapestry of love, reminding us that each moment is a precious gift.

What memories do you treasure most from family celebrations, and how can you pass those blessings on to the younger generations?

PRAYER

Dear Lord, thank You for the gift of family and the joy found in our gatherings. Help us to cherish these moments and to instill love and togetherness in our lives every day.

A family celebration is not just an event but a tapestry of love that weaves generations together.

THE GIFT OF A FAMILY HEIRLOOM

"See what kind of love the Father has given to us, that we should be called children of God." 1 John 3:1a

DEVOTIONAL

The greatest treasures we pass on are not found in gold or silver, but in the stories and love we share as family.

What cherished items have been passed down in your family, and how do they hold special meaning for you and your loved ones?

PRAYER

Heavenly Father, thank You for the treasures we hold from our loved ones. May we cherish these heirlooms, both for their beauty and the stories they carry, and may they remind us of the love that binds our families together.

Every heirloom tells a story, weaving our past
into the fabric of our present.

THE JOY OF A FAMILY PICNIC

"Let us come before his presence with thanksgiving; let us make a joyful noise to him with songs of praise!" Psalm 95:2

DEVOTIONAL

The laughter and love shared in simple moments can weave the strongest bonds within a family.

What fond memories do you have of family picnics, and how can you create new ones that bring joy to your loved ones today?

PRAYER

Dear Lord, thank you for the gift of family and the joy of shared moments. Help us to create new memories together and to cherish each other as we gather around the picnic blanket.

Family is the picnic blanket under the sun,
where laughter blossoms and love is nourished.

THE BLESSING OF A FAMILY REUNION

"Though the mountains be shaken and the hills be removed, yet my unfailing love for you will not be shaken." Isaiah 54:10

DEVOTIONAL

Every gathering is a reminder that family is our greatest treasure, woven together by love, faith, and shared memories.

What memories does your family picnic evoke for you? How did those moments of joy and connection make you feel in your heart?

PRAYER

Dear Lord, thank you for the gift of family and joyous moments spent together. May each gathering be filled with laughter, love, and the warmth of your presence.

Family picnics are not just meals in the sun; they are heartstrings woven together in laughter and shared stories.

THE GIFT OF A FAMILY GAME NIGHT

"And above all these put on love, which binds everything together in perfect harmony." "Colossians 3:14

DEVOTIONAL

Game nights are more than just entertainment; they are opportunities to weave love and connection into the fabric of our family lives.

What are some of your favorite memories from times spent with your family playing games together, and how can you create more of those moments now?

PRAYER

Dear Lord, thank you for the gift of family and the joy that comes from sharing laughter and love in our homes. May each game night be a chance to bond, create memories, and deepen our connections.

Every laugh shared over a game brings us closer together.

THE POWER OF A FAMILY BLESSING

"The Lord bless you and keep you; the Lord make His face shine upon you and be gracious to you." **Numbers 6:24-25**

DEVOTIONAL

A family blessing spoken with love can leave an indelible mark on the hearts of generations.

What blessings have you bestowed upon your family, and how have those blessings shaped the bonds you share?

PRAYER

Dear Lord, thank You for the gift of family and the power of our words. Help us to speak life and love into the hearts of our loved ones, nurturing blessings that endure across generations.

A family blessing is a gentle whisper that echoes through time, shaping futures with words of love.

THE BLESSING OF A FAMILY GRADUATION

"May he give you the desire of your heart and make all your plans succeed." **Psalm 20:4**

DEVOTIONAL

Each graduation is a milestone that beckons us to celebrate the power of family and the dreams we nurture together.

What memories come to mind when you think of your family's milestones? How have you celebrated their successes, and how have those moments shaped your own faith and values?

PRAYER

Dear Lord, thank You for the joy of seeing our families grow and achieve their dreams. Help us to celebrate each graduation with grateful hearts and wisdom to guide the next generation.

Graduations are more than just caps and gowns; they are the cherished moments that weave our family stories together.

THE GIFT OF A FAMILY WEDDING

"And as you wish that others would do to you, do so to them."
Luke 6:31

DEVOTIONAL

Family is an unbreakable thread woven through time, gathering our stories, lessons, and legacies into a tapestry of love.

What special memories do you cherish from your own wedding day, and how do those moments shape your feelings as you celebrate your family's union?

PRAYER

Dear Lord, thank you for the gift of family and the love that binds us together. May each wedding bring joy and cherished memories, reminding us of the beauty of commitment.

Weddings are the beautiful threads that weave generations together in love.

THE JOY OF A FAMILY BIRTHDAY

"She is more precious than rubies; nothing you desire can compare with her. Long life is in her right hand; in her left hand are riches and honor."
Proverbs 3:15-16

DEVOTIONAL

May you always find joy in the simplest of birthday moments, knowing that love is the greatest gift you can give.

What special memory do you cherish from a family birthday celebration that brings you joy and warmth every time you think of it?

PRAYER

Dear Lord, thank You for the gift of family and the joy that birthdays bring. Help us to celebrate each moment together, treasuring the love and laughter we share.

Every family birthday is a reminder that love grows richer with every passing year.

REMEMBERING LOVED ONES

"Blessed are those who mourn, for they will be comforted."
Matthew 5:4

DEVOTIONAL

In remembering our loved ones, we find ways to bring their laughter and love into our present, weaving their legacy into our lives.

What memories bring a smile to your heart when you think of your loved ones who have passed? How can you honor their legacy in your life today?

PRAYER

Dear Lord, as we remember those we have loved and lost, fill our hearts with gratitude for the moments shared and the love that remains. Help us to cherish their memories and keep their spirit alive within our hearts.

Love never leaves us; it shines brightly in the memories we hold dear.

THE BLESSING OF A FAMILY BAPTISM

"And I will make with them a covenant of peace; it shall be an everlasting covenant with them." Ezekiel 37:26

DEVOTIONAL

Baptism is not just a ceremony; it is a profound blessing that weaves our family closer in faith and love, creating lasting bonds across generations.

What memories do you cherish from your own family's baptisms, and how have those moments shaped your understanding of faith and family today?

PRAYER

Dear Lord, thank you for the precious gift of family and the moments we share that draw us closer to You. Help us to celebrate each baptism as a beautiful affirmation of faith and love in our family.

Baptism is not just a ritual; it is the sacred embrace of family, faith, and new beginnings.

THE GIFT OF A FAMILY ANNIVERSARY

"Teach them to your children, talking about them when you sit at home and when you walk along the road, when you lie down and when you get up." Deuteronomy 11:19

DEVOTIONAL

The richness of family anniversaries offers a precious opportunity to reflect on the love that binds us together and motivates us to pass down that love through generations.

What memories does your family anniversary bring back for you, and how can those cherished moments inspire your relationships today?

PRAYER

Dear Lord, thank You for the gift of family and the love we share through the years. Help us to celebrate the memories and create new ones, embracing the joy and laughter that binds us together.

Each anniversary is a reminder that love
grows deeper with every shared moment.

MAY 28

THE POWER OF A FAMILY TRADITION

"Your people will rebuild the ancient ruins and will raise up the age-old foundations; you will be called Repairer of Broken Walls, Restorer of Streets with Dwellings." Isaiah 58:12

DEVOTIONAL

Cherish your family traditions, for they create a tapestry of memories and faith that binds generations together.

What family tradition brings you joy and connection with your loved ones? How can you nurture and share this tradition to strengthen your family bond?

PRAYER

Dear God, thank You for the beautiful tapestry of family traditions. Help me to cherish and pass down those moments that strengthen our love and connection. May my heart be filled with gratitude for each shared experience.

Traditions are the threads that weave our hearts together,
creating a fabric of love and memory.

THE BLESSING OF A FAMILY VACATION

"But Mary treasured up all these things and pondered them in her heart."
Luke 2:19

DEVOTIONAL

Cherish the moments spent together, for they weave the fabric of family
and create lifelong bonds.

*What memories from family vacations do you treasure most? How have these
moments shaped your family's love and connection over the years? Reflecting on this
can bring a wave of joy and gratitude.*

PRAYER

Dear Lord, thank you for the blessing of family and the joyful moments we
share together. May our days spent on vacation be filled with laughter,
love, and lasting memories that draw us closer to one another and to You.

Family vacations are like patches in the quilt of our lives,
each patch telling a story of love, laughter, and togetherness.

THE GIFT OF A FAMILY PHOTO ALBUM

"And we know that in all things God works for the good of those who love
him, who have been called according to his purpose." **Romans 8:28**

DEVOTIONAL

Let your family photo album be a celebration of God's faithfulness,
reminding you of His purpose in every season of life.

*What memories do you treasure most when you flip through the pages of your family
photo album? How do those moments connect you to your loved ones today?*

PRAYER

Dear Lord, thank you for the gift of family and the memories captured in
photographs. Help me to cherish each moment and share these memories
with those I love.

Each photo tells a story; each story enriches the tapestry of our family.

THE JOY OF A FAMILY MOVIE NIGHT

"The living, the living, they praise you, as I am doing today; parents tell their children about your faithfulness." Isaiah 38:19

DEVOTIONAL

Creating joyful traditions is a beautiful way to nurture love and faith within our families.

What memories do you cherish from family movie nights, and how can you create even more joyful moments with your loved ones in the future?

PRAYER

Dear Lord, thank you for the gift of family and the joy that comes from sharing moments together. May our gatherings be filled with laughter, love, and warmth, creating memories that last a lifetime.

Togetherness in simple moments creates a bond that lasts forever.

JUNE 1

WELCOMING SUMMER: GOD'S LIGHT

"When Jesus spoke again to the people, he said, 'I am the light of the world. Whoever follows me will never walk in darkness, but will have the light of life." John 8:12

DEVOTIONAL

As summer beckons with its warmth and light, let us open our hearts and homes to God's presence, allowing His love to shine in our families and communities.

What does the arrival of summer mean to you? How can you invite God's light into your daily rhythms during this warm season? Reflect on the moments when you feel His presence the strongest.

PRAYER

Dear Lord, as the summer sun shines brightly, may Your love and light fill our hearts. Help us embrace the warmth of this season, drawing closer to You and to one another. Amen.

Summer is a reminder that God's light fills our lives
with warmth, beauty, and endless possibilities.

JUNE 2

THE BLESSING OF A FAMILY ROAD TRIP

"Be completely humble and gentle; be patient, bearing with one another in love. Make every effort to keep the unity of the Spirit through the bond of peace." Ephesians 4:2-3

DEVOTIONAL

Family trips may be filled with bumps along the road, but these moments teach us the deeper lessons of love, patience, and connection.

What memories come to mind when you think of family road trips from your own journey as a mother or grandmother? How have those experiences shaped your relationships with your loved ones?

PRAYER

Dear Lord, thank You for the gift of family and the joy of shared journeys. May our time together be filled with laughter, love, and cherished memories that draw us closer to one another and to You.

Every mile traveled together weaves a thread
in the tapestry of family love.

THE GIFT OF A FAMILY BARBECUE

"For where your treasure is, there your heart will be also."
Luke 12:34

DEVOTIONAL

The greatest treasures are not found in material things, but in the love, laughter, and memories we create with our family.

What special memories do you cherish from family gatherings, and how can you create new ones at your next barbecue?

PRAYER

Dear God, thank you for the gift of family and the joy they bring to our lives. May our gatherings be filled with laughter, love, and cherished moments.

Family gatherings are the threads that weave the fabric of our lives.

THE JOY OF A FAMILY HIKE

"In all your ways acknowledge Him, and He will make straight your paths."
Proverbs 3:6

DEVOTIONAL

Life's simplest adventures can deepen the bonds of family and remind us of the joy found in togetherness.

What moments do you cherish most when you're surrounded by your family on a nature hike? How do these times nurture your spirit and take you back to simpler days?

PRAYER

Dear Lord, thank you for the gift of family and the beauty of nature that surrounds us. May each step we take together strengthen our bonds and fill our hearts with joy.

Nature teaches us patience and reminds us
of the importance of living in the moment.

THE BLESSING OF A FAMILY CAMPOUT

"He will yet fill your mouth with laughter and your lips with shouting."
Job 8:21

DEVOTIONAL

In the quietness of family campouts, we discover that sometimes the simplest moments bring the richest blessings.

What special memories do you cherish from family outings, and how can you create new ones during your next family campout?

PRAYER

Dear Lord, thank You for the blessing of family and the memories we make together. Help us to cherish each moment spent under the stars and in the embrace of nature. May our hearts be filled with joy and laughter as we gather together.

In the glow of the campfire, family bonds are kindled anew.

THE GIFT OF A FAMILY POOL DAY

"Then they can urge the younger women to love their husbands and children, to be self-controlled and pure, to be busy at home, to be kind, and to be subject to their husbands, so that no one will malign the word of God." **Titus 2:4-5**

DEVOTIONAL

Cherish the moments spent with family, for they are gifts that enrich our lives and create bonds that last a lifetime.

What memories do you cherish most from family days spent by the pool, and how can you create new ones this summer?

PRAYER

Dear Lord, thank You for the gift of family and the joy of spending time together. Help us to cherish each moment, laughing and connecting as we enjoy the warmth of the sun and the love of one another.

Family time is not just an activity; it's a creation
of lasting memories woven through laughter and love.

JUNE 7

THE POWER OF A FAMILY PRAYER CIRCLE

"Rejoice always, pray continually, give thanks in all circumstances; for this is God's will for you in Christ Jesus." 1 Thessalonians 5:16-18

DEVOTIONAL

The power of prayer in our families creates a sacred space where love flourishes and connections deepen.

What memories do you cherish from the moments spent in prayer with your family? How have those experiences shaped your understanding of love and unity within your household?

PRAYER

Dear Lord, thank You for the gift of family and the bond that prayer creates among us. Help us to gather in Your presence, sharing our hearts, hopes, and dreams as we grow closer together.

Prayer is the thread that weaves our hearts together in love and grace.

JUNE 8

THE BLESSING OF A FAMILY GRADUATION

"Wisdom is the principal thing; therefore get wisdom: and with all thy getting get understanding." Proverbs 4:7

DEVOTIONAL

In every graduation, we are reminded that our nurturing spirit leaves a lasting legacy, encouraging our family to keep reaching for their dreams.

What memories do you cherish most from your own graduation or those of your loved ones, and how have they shaped your family legacy?

PRAYER

Dear Lord, thank You for the special milestone of graduation, for the joy it brings our families, and the memories we create together. May this season be filled with pride, love, and gratitude for all the hard work and dedication that has led to this moment.

Every graduation is a reminder of the countless seeds of love and wisdom we've sown in our family's journey.

THE GIFT OF A FAMILY FATHER'S DAY

"Honor your father and mother, which is the first commandment with a promise, so that it may go well with you and that you may enjoy long life on the earth." Ephesians 6:2-3

DEVOTIONAL

The greatest legacy we can offer is the love that honors those who came before us, weaving their stories into the fabric of our family.

What are some of your favorite memories of the moments you've shared with your family, and how do they reflect the love and wisdom you've passed down through the generations?

PRAYER

Dear Lord, thank you for the gift of family. Help us to treasure our time together and to cherish the love that binds us, today and always.

Family is not just an important thing; it is everything.

THE JOY OF A FAMILY FATHER FIGURE

"Fathers, do not provoke your children to anger, but bring them up in the discipline and instruction of the Lord." Ephesians 6:4

DEVOTIONAL

As grandmothers, we see how the loving guidance of a father figure can bring immense joy, not only to children but to the entire family.

What is one way you have experienced the comforting presence of a father figure in your life, and how can you emulate that warmth within your family today?

PRAYER

Dear Lord, thank You for the fathers and father figures who have blessed our lives with love and guidance. Help us to share that same spirit of joy and protection with our families, reflecting Your infinite love.

Joy flourishes in the garden of love,
where every family member is a cherished bloom.

JUNE 11

THE BLESSING OF A FAMILY GRANDFATHER

"But the lovingkindness of the Lord is from everlasting to everlasting on those who fear Him, and His righteousness to children's children."
Psalm 103:17

DEVOTIONAL

Family is a legacy, and each shared moment weaves a tapestry of love and wisdom that honors our ancestors and nurtures our grandchildren.

What are some cherished memories you have of your grandfather or of being a grandmother that remind you of the legacy of love in your family?

PRAYER

Dear Lord, thank you for the gift of family and the blessings that come with it. Help us to embrace and nurture our connections, creating a loving legacy for generations to come.

Love woven through generations is the greatest gift we can pass on.

JUNE 12

THE GIFT OF A FAMILY FATHER'S BLESSING

"Houses and wealth are inherited from parents, but a prudent wife is from the Lord." **Proverbs 19:14**

DEVOTIONAL

May you see the richness of your family blessings, knowing that your gentle guidance and loving presence are the most precious gifts you pass on to your loved ones.

What does the Father's blessing mean for your family, and how might you share that blessing with your loved ones today?

PRAYER

Dear God, thank you for the gift of family and the blessings that flow from Your love. Help me be a source of encouragement and grace within my family, reflecting Your heart in all our interactions.

A father's blessing echoes in a family's heart,
nurturing love and unity in every generation.

THE POWER OF A FAMILY FATHER'S PRAYER

"And that the prayer of faith will save the one who is sick, and the Lord will raise him up. And if he has committed sins, he will be forgiven."
James 5:15

DEVOTIONAL

Never underestimate the power of your prayers; they create a legacy of love, faith, and hope for your family.

What is one way you can invite the power of prayer into your family life today? How might a simple prayer shift the atmosphere in your home?

PRAYER

Dear Lord, thank you for the gift of family. Help me to lift my loved ones up in prayer daily, trusting in Your love and guidance over their lives.

Every whisper of prayer we send into the world is a thread that weaves our family closer to the heart of God.

JUNE 14

PRAYING FOR OUR COUNTRY

"I urge, then, first of all, that petitions, prayers, intercession, and thanksgiving be made for all people— for kings and all those in authority."
1 Timothy 2:1-2

DEVOTIONAL

Remember, dear one, that your prayers can be a powerful legacy that guides our country toward hope and peace.

What are your hopes and dreams for our country as you reflect on its past and future today?

PRAYER

Dear Lord, we come before you with grateful hearts for the land we call home. Please guide our leaders and unite us in love and understanding as we seek your will for our nation.

United in prayer, we can create a tapestry of hope for our country.

THE BLESSING OF A FAMILY FATHER'S LOVE

"For you are our Father, though Abraham does not know us and Israel does not acknowledge us; you, Lord, are our Father, our Redeemer from of old is your name." Isaiah 63:16

DEVOTIONAL

What a treasured gift it is to see the fruits of family, nurtured by a father's love, being passed down through generations.

What are some ways you've seen the love of a father reflected in your family, and how has that shaped your own understanding of love?

PRAYER

Dear Lord, thank You for the gift of family and for the depth of love we find in our relationships. Help us to recognize and cherish the blessings of a father's love in our lives.

Love weaves the fabric of our families, connecting generations with threads of understanding and warmth

JUNE 16

HONORING FATHERS

"Fathers, do not embitter your children, or they will become discouraged." Colossians 3:21

DEVOTIONAL

Honoring our fathers means cherishing and recognizing their contributions to our lives, keeping their legacy alive in the hearts of our children and grandchildren.

What memories do you cherish most about your father's influence in your life? How have those lessons shaped the way you love your family today?

PRAYER

Dear God, thank you for the fathers who have guided us with love and wisdom. May we honor them today by carrying forward their lessons in our hearts.

Love's legacy flows through generations, weaving the fabric of family stories.

THE GIFT OF A FAMILY FATHER'S WISDOM

"The wise woman builds her house, but with her own hands, the foolish one tears hers down." Proverbs 14:1

DEVOTIONAL

The greatest legacy we can leave our families is the wisdom we share through our love and life experiences.

What wisdom from your own father or father figure has shaped the way you nurture your family today? How can you share this legacy with those you love in a meaningful way?

PRAYER

Dear Lord, thank you for the gift of family and the wisdom that flows through generations. Help us to cherish and share this wisdom with those we love, nurturing a legacy of love and understanding.

Every moment spent sharing wisdom is a moment that strengthens the bonds of family.

THE JOY OF A FAMILY FATHER'S EXAMPLE

"Endure hardship as discipline; God is treating you as His children. For what children are not disciplined by their father?" Hebrews 12:7

DEVOTIONAL

The wisdom of a loving educator—be it a father, grandmother, or mentor —teaches us that growth often comes through challenges.

What wisdom from your own father or father figure has shaped the way you nurture your family today? How can you share this legacy with those you love in a meaningful way?

PRAYER

Dear Lord, thank you for the gift of family and the wisdom that flows through generations. Help us to cherish and share this wisdom with those we love, nurturing a legacy of love and understanding.

Every moment spent sharing wisdom is a moment that strengthens the bonds of family.

JUNE 19

FREEDOM AND FAITH

"The Spirit of the Lord is upon me, because He has anointed me to proclaim good news to the poor. He has sent me to proclaim freedom for the prisoners and recovery of sight for the blind, to set the oppressed free."
Luke 4:18

DEVOTIONAL

True freedom comes when we embrace love and trust in God, allowing us to break the chains that hinder our hearts.

What does freedom mean to you, and how has your faith guided you in understanding and embracing that freedom in your life? Reflect on moments when you've felt truly free and how those experiences have shaped your relationship with God and others.

PRAYER

Dear Lord, thank you for the gift of freedom and the faith that sustains us. Help us to embrace our past with gratitude and our future with hope, knowing that Your love knows no bounds.

True freedom is found in the grace of knowing
we are loved and valued by God.

JUNE 20

THE BLESSING OF A FAMILY SUMMER TRADITION

"Again, truly I tell you that if two of you on earth agree about anything they ask for, it will be done for them by my Father in heaven. For where two or three gather in my name, there am I with them." Matthew 18:19-20

DEVOTIONAL

In the warmth of family traditions, we weave bonds of love that reflect God's presence in our lives.

What is one special family tradition you've cherished over the years, and how has it drawn your loved ones closer together?

PRAYER

Dear Lord, thank you for the gift of family and the memories we create together. May we embrace our traditions, knowing they weave our hearts closer and fill our homes with joy.

Traditions are the threads that bind generations,
creating a tapestry of love and memories.

FIRST DAY OF SUMMER: GOD'S CREATION

"Lift up your eyes and look at the fields! They are ripe for harvest."
John 4:35

DEVOTIONAL

Each day, cherish God's creation, nurture family with patience, and, rooted in faith, grow in love—blooming with joy through every season.

What special moments in nature have you experienced that remind you of God's loving presence in your life? How can you incorporate those memories into your everyday routine this summer?

PRAYER

Dear Heavenly Father, as we step into the warmth of summer, help us to see Your handiwork all around us. May our hearts be filled with gratitude for the beauty of creation and the gift of every day.

Just as the sun rises each morning,
so does God's love renew in our lives.

JUNE 22

THE GIFT OF A FAMILY SUMMER PICNIC

"Kind words are like honey, sweet to the soul and healthy for the body."
Proverbs 16:24

DEVOTIONAL

Family picnics are a beautiful reminder that love and connection flourish in the simple moments we share together.

What does gathering your family around a picnic table mean to you, and how does it bring you joy and connection with your loved ones?

PRAYER

Dear Lord, thank you for the blessing of family and the memories we create together. May our hearts always be open to the love and laughter that these moments bring.

Every picnic is a promise kept, a memory in the making,
and love shared under the sun.

THE POWER OF A FAMILY SUMMER ADVENTURE

"For the Lord gives wisdom; from his mouth come knowledge and understanding." **Proverbs 2:6**

DEVOTIONAL

Cherish the simple adventures with your family, for they are the threads that weave lasting memories and strengthen bonds.

What adventure awaits your family this summer that could create lasting memories and deepen your bonds? How can you encourage each generation to share their stories and experiences during this precious time together?

PRAYER

Dear Lord, thank you for the gift of family and the joy of spending time together this summer. May our adventures bring us closer and allow us to share in laughter and love.

Every shared moment becomes a thread
in the beautiful tapestry of family.

JUNE 24

THE BLESSING OF A FAMILY SUMMER GARDEN

"But he answered them, 'My mother and my brothers are those who hear the word of God and do it." **Luke 8:21**

DEVOTIONAL

Every moment spent nurturing a garden is a love letter written to our family that continues to bloom with each season of our lives.

What memories does your family garden bring to mind, and how can those moments deepen your connections with your loved ones this summer?

PRAYER

Dear Lord, thank you for the beauty of nature and the joy it brings to our families. Help us to cherish the moments we share in our gardens, nurturing both plants and relationships alike.

Every seed sown in love can bloom into a cherished memory.

JUNE 25

THE GIFT OF A FAMILY SUMMER MEMORY

"And they shall be like a tree planted by the waters, that spreads out its roots by the river, and will not fear when the heat comes, for its leaves will be green, and it will not be anxious in the year of drought, nor will cease from yielding fruit." Jeremiah 17:8

DEVOTIONAL
Family is the garden of joy we tend to, where every moment spent together flowers into a cherished memory.

What summer memory do you cherish most with your family, and how did it shape your relationships with your loved ones?

PRAYER
Dear Lord, thank You for the gift of family and the memories we've created together. Help us to cherish each moment and pass down the love and joy that unites us.

Family memories are treasures that warm
the heart and bring us closer together.

JUNE 26

THE JOY OF A FAMILY SUMMER EVENING

"May our sons in their youth be like plants full grown, our daughters like corner pillars cut for the structure of a palace." Psalm 144:12

DEVOTIONAL
In the tapestry of family life, it is in these idyllic moments that we realize our love is the thread that holds us all together.

What are the small moments during summer evenings that bring you joy and remind you of the love within your family?

PRAYER
Dear Lord, thank You for the gift of family and the warmth of summer nights spent together. May our hearts always find joy in these precious moments, and may we cherish the laughter and love that fill the air.

Every summer evening spent with family
is a gentle reminder of love that lingers in the heart.

JUNE 27

THE BLESSING OF A FAMILY SUMMER STORM

"His faithfulness will be your shield and rampart."
Psalm 91:4

DEVOTIONAL

When storms come, they often clear the air and help us appreciate the sunny days, deepening our bonds and nurturing our connections.

What memories do you cherish from summer storms with your family, and how did those moments deepen your connections with one another?

PRAYER

Dear Lord, thank you for the beautiful ties of family and the joyful memories created even in tumultuous times. Help us to embrace each moment, rain or shine, as a gift of love and growth.

Sometimes the most beautiful moments
arise from the storms we weather together.

JUNE 28

THE GIFT OF A FAMILY SUMMER SUNSET

"His mercy extends to those who fear him, from generation to generation."
Luke 1:50

DEVOTIONAL

Cherish the fleeting moments spent with family, for they bring warmth and beauty to our lives like a summer sunset.

What memories do you cherish most from summer evenings spent with your family? How do they remind you of the love that surrounds you?

PRAYER

Dear Lord, thank you for the gift of family and the beauty of summer sunsets that remind us of Your love. May we cherish these moments together and hold them close to our hearts.

Every sunset we share is a reminder of the love that lights our lives.

JUNE 29

THE POWER OF A FAMILY SUMMER BLESSING

"Now to him who is able to do immeasurably more than all we ask or imagine, according to his power that is at work within us." Ephesians 3:20

DEVOTIONAL

In the heart of every summer blessing lies the truth that small gatherings can foster immeasurable love and connection across generations.

What are some ways you can bless your family this summer, creating moments of joy and connection that will be cherished for years to come?

PRAYER

Dear Lord, thank You for the gift of family. Please bless our time together this summer, filling our days with love, laughter, and lasting memories. Help us to cherish these moments and share Your light with one another.

Every shared moment is a thread
that weaves our family's tapestry of love.

JUNE 30

THE BLESSING OF A FAMILY SUMMER REFLECTION

"For I have chosen him, so that he will direct his children and his household after him to keep the way of the Lord by doing what is right and just, so that the Lord will bring about for Abraham what he has promised him." " Genesis 18:19

DEVOTIONAL

Cherish the beautiful moments spent together, for in them lies the grace of passing on love and faith to the next generation.

What special moments from this past summer with your family have deepened your appreciation for them? Take a moment to reflect on the laughter, love, and lessons shared. How can you carry those blessings into the seasons ahead?

PRAYER

Dear Lord, thank You for the gift of family and the joy they bring to our lives. May we always cherish the memories made together and find ways to nurture those bonds. Help us to treasure each moment, both big and small.

Family is the tapestry of our lives, woven together
with love, laughter, and shared memories.

Halfway Through Our Journey

You are now halfway through this devotional journey.

Many women discover this book through the thoughtful reviews shared by readers like you.

If these pages have supported your faith and daily reflection, would you consider sharing a short review on Amazon?

Your voice may help someone else find encouragement today.

devo.anchoredgraces.com/grandma

JULY 1

THE BLESSING OF FREEDOM

"So if the Son sets you free, you will be free indeed."
John 8:36

DEVOTIONAL

True freedom is found in knowing and sharing the depth of His love and grace with our families.

What does freedom mean to you in this season of your life, and how can you embrace it more fully each day?

PRAYER

Dear Lord, thank you for the gift of freedom that resides in our hearts. Help us to cherish and recognize the blessings that come with it, guiding our spirits towards joy and peace.

True freedom is found in the embrace of love and faith.

JULY 2

THE GIFT OF A FAMILY FIREWORKS NIGHT

"For I know the plans I have for you," declares the Lord, "plans to prosper you and not to harm you, plans to give you hope and a future."
Jeremiah 29:11

DEVOTIONAL

The sweetest fireworks are not found in the sky, but in the cherished moments we share with our loved ones.

What special memories does your family bring to mind when you think of joyful celebrations, and how can you cultivate those moments even more?

PRAYER

Dear Lord, thank you for the precious gift of family. May our hearts be filled with love and gratitude as we gather together to create beautiful memories under the night sky.

Family is the spark that ignites our hearts
and lightens the darkness of the night.

THE JOY OF A FAMILY BARBECUE

"But as for me and my household, we will serve the Lord."
Joshua 24:15

DEVOTIONAL

Family gatherings are more than simply cooking and sharing food; they are a joyful celebration of the bonds that God has blessed us with, highlighting the importance of unity and love in our homes.

What memories does your family barbecue bring to mind, and how have they shaped your relationships with those you love most?

PRAYER

Dear Lord, thank you for the warmth of family gatherings and the joy they bring to our hearts. May each moment shared around the grill be filled with laughter and love, drawing us closer to one another and to You.

Family is the grill that brings sizzling joy to our hearts,
flavored by love and laughter.

THANKFUL FOR FREEDOM

"He has sent me to bind up the brokenhearted, to proclaim freedom for the captives and release from darkness for the prisoners." Isaiah 61:1

DEVOTIONAL

Let gratitude and love fill your heart, for in both freedom and family, we see the tender hand of God at work.

What does freedom mean to you in this season of your life, and how can you express gratitude for the independence you cherish?

PRAYER

Dear Lord, thank you for the gift of freedom in our lives—freedom to love, to share, and to grow. Help us to appreciate each moment of independence and to use it wisely to serve you and those we love.

Freedom is not just a privilege; it's a beautiful responsibility
filled with choices and opportunities.

JULY 5

THE BLESSING OF A FAMILY PARADE

"Children are a heritage from the Lord, offspring a reward from him."
Psalm 127:3

DEVOTIONAL
The greatest treasures in our lives often come not wrapped in ribbon but in the moments of shared joy and laughter with our loved ones.

What does the story of your family's journey look like, and how can you celebrate each member's unique contribution in your 'family parade'?

PRAYER
Dear Lord, thank You for the beautiful family You've woven into my life. Help me to cherish the moments we share and to see Your hand in the diversity of our bonds.

In the parade of life, every family member brings their own colors to the canvas of our shared experience.

JULY 6

THE GIFT OF A FAMILY SUMMER DAY

"Let your light shine before others, that they may see your good deeds and glorify your Father in heaven." **Matthew 5:16**

DEVOTIONAL
Relish in the precious gift of family time, for it is a divine blessing that enriches hearts across generations.

What are some of your favorite memories spent with family during the summer, and how can you create new moments that bless everyone around you?

PRAYER
Dear Lord, thank You for the gift of family and the joy of summer days spent together. Help us to cherish these moments and create lasting memories filled with love and laughter.

Family is the heart of our summer,
where love blooms in the warmth of togetherness.

JULY 7

THE POWER OF A FAMILY SUMMER PRAYER

"Delight yourself in the Lord, and He will give you the desires of your heart." Psalm 37:4

DEVOTIONAL

The power of family prayer can create cherished moments of connection, drawing our loved ones closer together in faith and love.

What memories do you cherish that were woven into the fabric of summer gatherings with your family, and how can you invite the power of prayer into those moments this season?

PRAYER

Dear Lord, as the warmth of summer wraps around us, we thank You for the gift of family. May our hearts unite in prayer, filling our time together with love, joy, and peace.

Through prayer, we cultivate bonds that last beyond the seasons.

JULY 8

THE BLESSING OF A FAMILY SUMMER OUTING

"These commandments that I give you today are to be on your hearts. Impress them on your children. Talk about them when you sit at home and when you walk along the road, when you lie down and when you get up." Deuteronomy 6:6-7

DEVOTIONAL

Every family outing is a beautiful opportunity to bond, teach, and share God's love across generations.

What special memories do you hold from past family summer outings, and how can you create new ones that your loved ones will cherish?

PRAYER

Dear Lord, thank you for the gift of family. May our time together this summer be filled with joy, laughter, and love, as we create beautiful memories that bind our hearts closer to one another.

Family time is a treasure that enriches our souls and weaves the fabric of love.

THE GIFT OF A FAMILY SUMMER CRAFT

"A generous person will prosper; whoever refreshes others will be refreshed." **Proverbs 11:25**

DEVOTIONAL

In every project we share with our families, we weave threads of love that strengthen our bonds and fill our hearts.

What crafts or activities have brought your family together during the summers? Can you recall a special moment when laughter and creativity filled the air?

PRAYER

Dear Lord, thank you for the gift of family and the joy that comes from creating together. Please bless our time spent in craft and creativity, enriching our bonds and filling our hearts with love.

Crafting together weaves threads of love that bind our hearts for a lifetime.

JULY 10

THE JOY OF A FAMILY SUMMER GAME

"He who finds a wife finds what is good and receives favor from the Lord." **Proverbs 18:22**

DEVOTIONAL

Creating joyful memories with family ignites a deeper love that will warm our hearts for years to come.

What special memories do you cherish from summers spent playing games with your family? How can you create new joyful moments together this year?

PRAYER

Dear Lord, thank you for the gift of family and the laughter we share together. Help us to cherish these moments and create lasting memories that bring us closer to one another.

Joy blooms in every shared game,
echoing love from generation to generation.

JULY 11

THE BLESSING OF A FAMILY SUMMER TRADITION

"Let your roots grow down into Him, and let your lives be built on Him."
Colossians 2:7

DEVOTIONAL

In nurturing such traditions, we cultivate an environment of love, connection, and belonging, where each family member feels valued and cherished.

What cherished family tradition do you look forward to every summer, and how does it deepen your bond with your loved ones?

PRAYER

Dear Lord, thank You for the gift of family and the memories we create together. May this summer be filled with laughter, love, and lasting connections.

Traditions are the threads that weave our families together, creating a tapestry of love and memories.

JULY 12

THE GIFT OF A FAMILY SUMMER RECIPE

"Train up a child in the way he should go; even when he is old he will not depart from it." **Proverbs 22:6**

DEVOTIONAL

The recipes we share become more than just instructions; they serve as a bridge connecting the past, present, and future of our family.

What family recipe brings back cherished memories and reminds you of the love shared around the dinner table? How can you pass that gift along to your loved ones this summer?

PRAYER

Dear Lord, thank you for the precious bonds of family and the meals shared together. May each gathering around the table deepen our love and strengthen our connections. Bless our kitchens with joy and laughter as we prepare our favorite dishes.

Food is love served on a plate, feeding both body and soul.

JULY 13

THE POWER OF A FAMILY SUMMER BLESSING

"Forget not all his benefits."
Psalm 103:2

DEVOTIONAL

Cherish the moments spent together, for in family, we find our greatest blessings.

What memories do you cherish most about summers spent with your family, and how can you create new blessings during this season together?

PRAYER

Dear Lord, thank you for the gift of family and the joy of summer days together. May our gatherings be filled with love, laughter, and blessings that bind our hearts closer to each other and to You.

Summer is a tapestry woven with the threads of love, laughter, and togetherness.

JULY 14

THE BLESSING OF A FAMILY SUMMER MEMORY

"By wisdom a house is built, and by understanding it is established; and by knowledge the rooms are filled with all precious and pleasant riches."
Proverbs 24:3-4

DEVOTIONAL

Every moment spent with family is a precious thread woven into the tapestry of our lives.

What cherished summer memory with your family brings a smile to your heart? How can you nurture those bonds today?

PRAYER

Dear Lord, thank You for the beautiful memories we've created with our loved ones. Help us to cherish these moments and continue to foster love within our families, drawing us closer together in joy.

Family is the golden thread that weaves our hearts together.

THE GIFT OF A FAMILY SUMMER ADVENTURE

"Consequently, you are no longer foreigners and strangers, but fellow citizens with God's people and also members of his household,"
Ephesians 2:19

DEVOTIONAL

Family adventures not only create lasting memories but also strengthen the bonds we cherish most in our hearts.

What is one cherished memory from a family summer adventure that brought you closer to your loved ones? How can you create a new memory this year?

PRAYER

Dear Lord, thank You for the beautiful gift of family and the joy of shared adventures. Help us to cherish these moments together and build lasting memories that honor Your love.

Family adventures are not just about the destination,
but about the hearts that journey together.

JULY 16

THE JOY OF A FAMILY SUMMER EVENING

"Rejoice in the Lord always; again I will say, rejoice."
Philippians 4:4

DEVOTIONAL

Never underestimate the joyful power of family connections; they are the roots that nourish our soul.

What are some of your favorite memories of summer evenings spent with your family, and how can you create new moments together this season?

PRAYER

Dear Lord, thank You for the gift of family and the warmth of summer evenings. As we gather together, may we cherish each laugh, story, and moment shared, and may Your love surround us all.

Every gathering we share is a thread woven
into the tapestry of our family's love.

THE BLESSING OF A FAMILY SUMMER STORM

"Therefore everyone who hears these words of mine and puts them into practice is like a wise man who built his house on the rock." Matthew 7:24

DEVOTIONAL
Sometimes the storms of life bring us closer to the ones we love, reminding us of the strength found in unity and shared moments.

What storms have you experienced in your family life that have ultimately brought you closer together? How have you seen your loved ones grow through challenges?

PRAYER
Dear Heavenly Father, thank You for the bonds that hold our families together, especially during the storms. Help us to see the beauty in the chaos, reminding us that through struggle comes strength and unity.

Just as a summer storm refreshes the earth, so do the trials in our lives nurture deeper connections within our families.

JULY 18

THE GIFT OF A FAMILY SUMMER SUNSET

"The Lord will guide you always; he will satisfy your needs in a sun-scorched land and will strengthen your frame. You will be like a well-watered garden, like a spring whose waters never fail." Isaiah 58:11

DEVOTIONAL
Cherish the simple moments with family, for they are the true treasures that light up our lives.

What are some cherished memories you've created with your family during summer sunsets that still bring a smile to your heart?

PRAYER
Dear Lord, thank you for the gift of family and the beauty of summer sunsets. Help us to cherish these moments together, nurturing love and joy in our hearts.

The warmth of a summer sunset reflects the love that binds our families together.

THE POWER OF A FAMILY SUMMER REFLECTION

"For where two or three gather in my name, there am I with them."
Matthew 18:20

DEVOTIONAL

Cherish the time spent with family, for it is in those moments that you cultivate love, faith, and lasting memories.

What cherished moments from past summers with your family bring a smile to your heart? How can you carry those memories forward to create new ones this year?

PRAYER

Dear Father, we thank You for the gift of family and the love that binds us. Help us to cherish our time together and to create lasting memories this summer. May Your presence fill our hearts with joy and gratitude.

Every family gathering is a treasure trove of love waiting to be explored.

JULY 20

THE BLESSING OF A FAMILY SUMMER GATHERING

"Behold, how good and pleasant it is when brothers dwell in unity!"
Psalm 133:1

DEVOTIONAL

Family thrives in love and laughter, and it is in gatherings that we nourish this bond and keep our roots strong.

What are some cherished memories from past family gatherings that bring a smile to your heart, and how can you create new ones this summer?

PRAYER

Dear Lord, thank you for the precious gift of family. May this summer gathering be filled with laughter, love, and lasting memories. Amen.

Every moment spent together is a thread
woven into the fabric of our family's love.

JULY 21

THE GIFT OF A FAMILY SUMMER PICNIC

"And all your children shall be taught by the Lord, and great shall be the peace of your children." Isaiah 54:13

DEVOTIONAL

The day holds within it the essence of unity and the joy of togetherness in Christ.

What special memories come to mind when you think about the picnics you've shared with your family? How can you create new moments this summer that will become cherished stories for generations to come?

PRAYER

Dear Lord, thank You for the family connections that enrich our lives. Help us to celebrate each moment together, sharing laughter and love in the simple joys of a summer picnic.

Family picnics are not just meals; they are heartbeats of love and laughter shared under the open sky.

JULY 22

THE JOY OF A FAMILY SUMMER HIKE

"My beloved is mine, and I am his. He feeds among the lilies." Song of Solomon 2:16

DEVOTIONAL

Find joy in every moment spent with family, for it is in these simple gatherings that God's love is most beautifully shared.

What memories do you cherish most from your family hikes, and how do they reflect the love and joy shared within your family?

PRAYER

Dear Lord, thank you for the beauty of nature and the gift of family. May our moments together be filled with laughter and love, deepening our bonds with each step.

Joy blooms in our hearts when we wander through nature with those we love.

THE BLESSING OF A FAMILY SUMMER CAMPOUT

"Therefore encourage one another and build each other up, just as in fact you are doing." 1 Thessalonians 5:11

DEVOTIONAL

In the beauty of togetherness, we find that time spent with family is one of life's greatest blessings.

What memories do you cherish most from family summer campouts, and how can you share those moments with your loved ones today?

PRAYER

Dear Heavenly Father, thank you for the gift of family and the joyful moments we share. Help us to create lasting memories and strengthen our bonds during these precious times together. Amen.

Gathered around the campfire, hearts ignite with laughter and love, weaving a tapestry of cherished memories.

THE GIFT OF A FAMILY SUMMER POOL DAY

"And let us not grow weary of doing good, for in due season we will reap, if we do not give up." Galatians 6:9

DEVOTIONAL

Never underestimate the joy of creating lasting memories with loved ones, for they are the threads that bind our family tapestry together.

What memories or lessons from your own family gatherings come to mind when you think about a summer pool day? How can you share the warmth of those moments with your loved ones now?

PRAYER

Dear Lord, thank you for the warmth of the sun and the laughter of family. Help us cherish these moments together and create memories that will last a lifetime.

Family is like the water we swim in;
it nourishes, refreshes, and connects us.

THE POWER OF A FAMILY SUMMER PRAYER

"And let us consider how we may spur one another on toward love and good deeds, not giving up meeting together, as some are in the habit of doing, but encouraging one another." Hebrews 10:24-25

DEVOTIONAL

In the chaos of life, a simple prayer with family can strengthen the love that binds us together.

What memories come to mind when you think of family summers spent together? How has prayer played a role in those moments, drawing your loved ones closer to one another and to God?

PRAYER

Dear Lord, thank You for the gift of family and the time we share together. May our summer gatherings be filled with laughter, love, and prayers that unite our hearts in faith.

Through prayer, we cultivate a garden where
love blossoms and family bonds deepen.

JULY 26

THE BLESSING OF A FAMILY SUMMER TRADITION

"To everything, there is a season,
and a time for every matter under heaven." Ecclesiastes 3:1

DEVOTIONAL

Through every season of family traditions, we find opportunities to cultivate love, joy, and connection that lasts for generations.

What cherished family tradition brings you the most joy during the summer months? How can you pass that warmth on to the younger generations in your family?

PRAYER

Dear Lord, thank you for the blessing of family and the moments we share together. We ask for your guidance to keep our summer traditions alive, allowing love and connection to flourish in every gathering.

Traditions are the thread that weaves our family story together.

THE GIFT OF A FAMILY SUMMER RECIPE

"Her children rise up and call her blessed; her husband also,
and he praises her." **Proverbs 31:28**

DEVOTIONAL

The heart of a family lies in the recipes we share, filled with laughter, love,
and the warmth of tradition.

*What cherished summer recipe from your family brings back the sweetest memories,
and how can you share that joy with your loved ones this season?*

PRAYER

Dear Lord, thank you for the gift of family and the memories we create
around the table. Help us to share our love and laughter through our
cherished recipes and the meals we prepare together.

Food binds our hearts as much as it fills our plates.

THE JOY OF A FAMILY SUMMER GAME

"And he will turn the hearts of the fathers to their children, and the hearts
of the children to their fathers." **Malachi 4:6**

DEVOTIONAL

The joy of family games not only strengthens bonds but also creates
cherished memories that fill our hearts with warmth for years to come.

*What special memories come to mind when you think about summer games with
your family? How do those moments of laughter and joy reflect the love that binds
your family together?*

PRAYER

Dear Lord, thank You for the gift of family and the joy found in simple
moments together. Help us to cherish these times and create memories
that will last a lifetime.

Joy is found in the shared laughter and togetherness
of our family moments.

THE BLESSING OF A FAMILY SUMMER MEMORY

"Children's children are a crown to the aged, and parents are the pride of their children." **Proverbs 17:6**

DEVOTIONAL

Cherish every moment spent with your family, for it is in these gatherings that love deepens and memories are woven into the fabric of our hearts.

What does family togetherness mean to you, and how have games created lasting memories in your life? As you consider this, think about a recent gathering where laughter filled the air.

PRAYER

Dear Lord, thank You for the joy of family and the laughter shared during our summer games. Help us to create precious moments that deepen our bonds and create memories to cherish.

Joy blossoms in the moments shared,
laughter echoing through our homes like sweet music.

JULY 30

THE GIFT OF A FAMILY SUMMER ADVENTURE

"Teach them to your children, talking about them when you sit at home and when you walk along the road, when you lie down and when you get up." **Deuteronomy 11:19**

DEVOTIONAL

The greatest treasure is not found in places we visit, but in the love we share along the journey.

What are some cherished memories of summer adventures you've shared with your family, and how can you create new ones this year?

PRAYER

Dear Lord, thank You for the gift of family and the beautiful adventures that bring us closer together. May our hearts be open to the joy and love that summer brings, creating lasting memories.

Every summer adventure is a thread woven
into the colorful tapestry of family life.

THE POWER OF A FAMILY SUMMER BLESSING

"My command is this: Love each other as I have loved you. Greater love has no one than this: to lay down one's life for one's friends."
John 15:12-13

DEVOTIONAL

The love we cultivate in our families during special times together stays with us, bridging generations and teaching us the essence of grace and connection.

What does the idea of a summer blessing mean to you and how can you share that blessing with your family this season?

PRAYER

Dear Lord, thank You for the gift of family and the joy of summer days together. May we be a source of love and blessing to one another, finding joy in every moment shared. Amen.

Family is like a garden; with love and nurturing, it blossoms beautifully.

THE BLESSING OF A NEW SCHOOL YEAR

"Every good and perfect gift is from above, coming down from the Father of the heavenly lights." James 1:17

DEVOTIONAL

Let us treasure the gift of new beginnings and the blessings that come hand in hand with each academic year.

What are some ways you can offer support and encouragement to the children and grandchildren in your life as they embark on a new school year?

PRAYER

Heavenly Father, thank You for the gift of a new school year full of possibilities. Help us to be a source of love and encouragement for our children and grandchildren as they learn and grow in Your grace.

Every new beginning holds the promise of new blessings.

AUGUST 2

THE GIFT OF A FAMILY BACK-TO-SCHOOL TRADITION

"Children's children are a crown to the aged, and parents are the pride of their children." Proverbs 17:6

DEVOTIONAL

This back-to-school tradition is a beautiful reminder that the moments we share today become the treasured stories our grandchildren will carry with them tomorrow.

What special traditions do you hold dear when it comes to your family's back-to-school season? How can you nurture and pass them on to the younger generations in your life?

PRAYER

Dear Lord, thank You for the gift of family and the opportunity to create cherished memories together. As the new school year begins, may our hearts be filled with love and gratitude for the time we share.

Traditions weave the fabric of our family history, connecting generations with love and laughter.

AUGUST 3

THE JOY OF A FAMILY SUMMER'S END

"My soul magnifies the Lord, and my spirit rejoices in God my Savior."
Luke 1:46-47

DEVOTIONAL

Let the joy of shared moments remind you to celebrate the love that binds your family together, for it brings light even as the seasons shift.

What cherished moments from this summer have filled your heart with joy, and how can you carry that warmth into the autumn months ahead?

PRAYER

Dear Lord, thank you for the gift of family and the memories we've created together this summer. Help us to weave those joyful moments into the fabric of our everyday lives as we embrace the beauty of change.

In the golden hues of autumn, may we gather the joy of summer and plant seeds of love for the seasons to come.

AUGUST 4

THE BLESSING OF A FAMILY SUMMER REFLECTION

"And God blessed them, and God said to them, 'Be fruitful and multiply and fill the earth and subdue it; and have dominion over the fish of the sea and over the birds of the heavens and over every living thing that moves on the earth.'" **Genesis 1:28**

DEVOTIONAL

The true blessing of family lies in the love that flows through generations, bringing joy and wisdom to each new chapter of life.

What family memories from this summer bring you the greatest joy? How can you cherish those moments and pass on their lessons to the next generation?

PRAYER

Dear Lord, thank You for the gift of family and the memories we create together. Help us to treasure each moment and to share our love and wisdom with those we hold dear.

Every shared laugh and story we cherish today plants the seeds of connection for tomorrow.

THE GIFT OF A FAMILY SUMMER MEMORY

"But the fruit of the Spirit is love, joy, peace, forbearance, kindness, goodness, faithfulness, gentleness and self-control." Galatians 5:22-23

DEVOTIONAL

As we nurture our families, let us cherish the ordinary moments, for they often become the most treasured memories.

What cherished moments from summers past with your family bring a smile to your heart? How do these memories shape your love for them today?

PRAYER

Dear Lord, we thank You for the gift of family and the beautiful memories we create together. May our hearts be filled with gratitude as we cherish these special times and look forward to making new ones.

Family is the canvas upon which we paint the colors of our memories.

THE POWER OF A FAMILY SUMMER BLESSING

"And they shall be mine, says the Lord of hosts, in that day when I make up my treasured possession." Malachi 3:17

DEVOTIONAL

The bonds we nurture with our families during the warm summer months can become an enduring legacy, providing joy and strength in every season of life.

What family traditions do you cherish the most during the summer months, and how can you share those blessings with the generations to come?

PRAYER

Dear Lord, thank You for the precious gift of family. Help me to embrace and celebrate the summer moments together, nurturing love, laughter, and togetherness in our hearts.

Family is not just an important thing; it is everything, especially during the seasons of joy.

THE BLESSING OF A FAMILY SUMMER GATHERING

"May your unfailing love be with us, Lord, even as we put our hope in you."
Psalm 33:22

DEVOTIONAL

Every summer gathering is a reminder that family is a treasure, rich in love and connection.

What memories do you cherish most from past summer gatherings with your family, and how can you invite those moments into this year's celebration?

PRAYER

Dear Lord, thank you for the gift of family and the joy that summer gatherings bring. May this time be filled with laughter and love, as we celebrate the blessing of togetherness.

Family is where life begins and love never ends.

THE GIFT OF A FAMILY SUMMER PICNIC

"Your wife will be like a fruitful vine within your house; your children will be like olive shoots around your table." **Psalm 128:3**

DEVOTIONAL

The simple joys of togetherness not only strengthen family ties but also enrich our souls with love and gratitude.

What memories does the idea of a family picnic evoke for you? How can you create new moments this summer that will be cherished by your loved ones for years to come?

PRAYER

Dear Lord, thank You for the families we cherish and the love that bonds us together. Please bless our gatherings with joy and laughter, creating lasting memories that warm our hearts.

Family picnics are not just meals; they are heartstrings woven together under the sun.

THE JOY OF A FAMILY SUMMER HIKE

"You are the light of the world. A city set on a hill cannot be hidden."
Matthew 5:14-16

DEVOTIONAL

Family time in nature is a gentle reminder that love grows best in shared experiences, nurturing bonds that last a lifetime.

What do you cherish most about the times you spend with your family during summertime picnics?

PRAYER

Dear Lord, thank you for the joyful moments spent together as a family. May each picnic be a reminder of the love, laughter, and memories we share. Bless our gatherings and fill our hearts with gratitude.

Moments of joy are the thread that weaves family together.

THE BLESSING OF A FAMILY SUMMER CAMPOUT

"Trust in the Lord with all your heart and lean not on your own understanding; in all your ways acknowledge Him, and He will make your paths straight." **Proverbs 3:5-6**

DEVOTIONAL

Cherish each moment spent with family, for they are the threads that create the rich tapestry of love and memories.

What cherished memories do you have of family gatherings under the stars, and how can you continue to create these moments of joy and connection with your loved ones?

PRAYER

Dear Lord, thank you for the gift of family and the simple joys of summer campouts. May our time together deepen our bonds and draw us closer to you.

Family is a tapestry woven with love, laughter, and memories that last a lifetime.

THE GIFT OF A FAMILY SUMMER POOL DAY

"She is more precious than rubies;
nothing you desire can compare with her" Proverbs 3:15

DEVOTIONAL

The laughter of loved ones by the pool is a precious reminder that family time is a beautiful gift, enriching our lives in ways that last forever.

What are the moments you've cherished most during family gatherings by the pool, and how can you reflect that joy into your grandchildren's lives today?

PRAYER

Dear God, thank you for the gift of family and the laughter shared during sunny pool days. May every splash remind us of your love and bring us closer together.

Water nurtures our bodies, but love nurtures our hearts.

THE POWER OF A FAMILY SUMMER PRAYER

"Listen, my son, to your father's instruction and do not forsake your mother's teaching. They are a garland to grace your head and a chain to adorn your neck." Proverbs 1:8-9

DEVOTIONAL

Let our summer prayers be an invitation to cultivate faith and love, reminding us of the profound impact our family carries through God's grace.

What hopes and dreams are you holding for your family this summer, and how can prayer help anchor those aspirations?

PRAYER

Dear Lord, as the warmth of summer surrounds us, we ask for your blessing on our family gatherings. May our hearts be open to love and understanding, and may your spirit guide our conversations and connections.

Prayer is the quiet, powerful thread
that weaves our family closer together.

THE BLESSING OF A FAMILY SUMMER TRADITION

"Let all that you do be done in love."
1 Corinthians 16:14

DEVOTIONAL

Family traditions, like summer barbecues, are reminders of the blessings God bestows upon us, providing joy and connection that anchore our families through every season of life.

What is one family summer tradition that brings you joy, and how can you intentionally pass on its significance to your loved ones this year?

PRAYER

Dear Lord, thank You for the blessings of family traditions that create cherished memories. Help us to nurture and share these moments with our loved ones, fostering love and connection.

Traditions are threads that weave our family's story together.

THE GIFT OF A FAMILY SUMMER RECIPE

"And he will turn the hearts of the fathers to their children, and the hearts of the children to their fathers, lest I come and strike the land with a decree of utter destruction." **Malachi 4:6**

DEVOTIONAL

In the embrace of family, we find our truest treasures and the sweetest joys are often stirred together, just like a well-loved recipe.

What is a cherished recipe that has been passed down through your family, and what memories does it bring to your heart?

PRAYER

Dear God, thank you for the blessing of family and the memories we create together. May this summer be filled with love, laughter, and delicious meals that bring us closer to one another.

Food made with love nourishes not just the body, but the soul.

AUGUST 15

THE JOY OF A FAMILY SUMMER GAME

"Praise the Lord! I will praise the Lord as long as I live; I will sing praises to my God while I have my being." Psalm 146:1-2

DEVOTIONAL

The warmth of family joy, just like a sunny summer's day, is best when shared and celebrated together.

What memories come to your mind when you think of summer games with your family? How does it feel to witness laughter and joy shared across generations?

PRAYER

Dear Lord, thank you for the gift of family and the joy that simple summer games bring. May our hearts be filled with laughter, and may these moments draw us closer to one another and to You.

Joy is best experienced in the company of those we love.

AUGUST 16

THE BLESSING OF A FAMILY SUMMER MEMORY

"Whatever you have learned or received or heard from me, or seen in me —practice these things, and the God of peace will be with you."
Philippians 4:9

DEVOTIONAL

Life teaches us that the simplest moments spent together create the most profound memories in our hearts.

What summer memories do you cherish the most with your family, and how have they shaped your relationships over the years?

PRAYER

Dear God, thank you for the gift of family and the precious memories we create together. Help us to cherish each moment and embrace new experiences with love and laughter.

Every family gathering is a thread woven
into the beautiful tapestry of our lives.

THE GIFT OF A FAMILY SUMMER ADVENTURE

"Each of you should use whatever gift you have received to serve others, as faithful stewards of God's grace in its various forms." **1 Peter 4:10**

DEVOTIONAL

Family creates a tapestry of love that enriches our lives and reminds us of the simple joys that God blesses us with.

What does a summer adventure with your family mean to you, and how can you foster those cherished moments together?

PRAYER

Dear Heavenly Father, thank you for the blessing of family. Help us to embrace each adventure as a treasured gift, creating memories that will last a lifetime.

Every adventure shared with family is a thread woven into the fabric of our hearts.

AUGUST 18

THE POWER OF A FAMILY SUMMER BLESSING

"Commit your way to the Lord; trust in him, and he will act." **Psalm 37:5**

DEVOTIONAL

Family love is a blessing that grows stronger as we nurture it with time, laughter, and shared moments.

What blessings can you bring to your family this summer, and how can you encourage others to share their blessings with you?

PRAYER

Dear Lord, thank you for the gift of family and the joys that summer brings. May we cherish our time together, sharing love and blessings freely among each other.

Family bonds are woven stronger with each shared blessing, creating a tapestry of love that lasts through generations.

THE BLESSING OF A FAMILY SUMMER REFLECTION

"A wise son brings joy to his father, but a foolish son brings grief to his mother." **Proverbs 10:1**

DEVOTIONAL

In reflecting on our family gatherings, let us remember that our presence and the love we share are the true blessings that shape generations.

What special moments with your family this summer fill your heart with joy? How can you foster a spirit of blessing and gratitude among your loved ones during this season?

PRAYER

Dear Lord, thank you for the beautiful gift of family. May we share laughter, love, and blessings with one another this summer, growing closer in your grace.

Every hug, every shared meal, and every story told is a thread in the tapestry of our family.

AUGUST 20

THE GIFT OF A FAMILY SUMMER GATHERING

"As a mother comforts her child, so will I comfort you." **Isaiah 66:13**

DEVOTIONAL

Every shared moment and every hug exchanged are like threads woven into the fabric of our family, creating a tapestry that tells our unique story.

What cherished memories do you hold close from summer gatherings with your family, and how can you create new ones this year?

PRAYER

Dear Lord, thank You for the gift of family. May our summer gatherings be filled with laughter, love, and precious moments that draw us closer together.

Family is the heart of our summers, where love blooms and laughter echoes.

AUGUST 21

THE JOY OF A FAMILY SUMMER PICNIC

"Enjoy life with the wife you love all the days of this meaningless life that God has given you under the sun—all your meaningless days. For this is your lot in life and in your toilsome labor under the sun." Ecclesiastes 9:9

DEVOTIONAL

Cherish each moment spent with family, for these simple gatherings create lasting memories that warm the heart for a lifetime.

What memories or traditions surface in your heart when you think of family picnics during the summer? How do these moments of connection fill your spirit with joy?

PRAYER

Dear Lord, thank you for the gift of family and the joyful moments we share together. May our summer picnics be filled with laughter, love, and cherished memories that draw us closer to one another and to You.

Joy is found in the laughter that dances between generations.

AUGUST 22

THE BLESSING OF A FAMILY SUMMER HIKE

"And He will be like a tree planted by the rivers of water, that brings forth its fruit in its season, whose leaf also shall not wither; and whatever he does shall prosper." Psalm 1:3

DEVOTIONAL

The richness of family days spent together, even in simple activities like hiking, can be a source of nourishment and strength for our spirits.

What memories do you cherish from summers spent hiking with your family, and how can you create new moments to enjoy together this year?

PRAYER

Dear Lord, thank you for the beauty of nature and the joy of family. Help us to create lasting memories this summer as we walk hand in hand along your creation.

Every step on the trail connects us not just to nature, but to each other.

AUGUST 23

THE GIFT OF A FAMILY SUMMER CAMPOUT

"For I know that my Redeemer lives, and at the last He will stand upon the earth." Job 19:25

DEVOTIONAL

Cherish every moment with your family, for it is in these gatherings that love is nurtured and memories are made.

What memories from past family gatherings fill your heart with joy, and how can you weave those moments into this summer's campout?

PRAYER

Dear Lord, thank you for the blessing of family. May this summer campout strengthen our bonds and create beautiful memories that draw us closer to You and each other.

Family is the heart of our happiness and the canvas of our memories.

AUGUST 24

THE POWER OF A FAMILY SUMMER POOL DAY

"I can do all things through Christ who strengthens me."
Philippians 4:13

DEVOTIONAL

The laughter shared during simple moments can be a reflection of love that binds our families together.

What joys and memories come to your mind when you think of summer days spent by the pool with your loved ones? How can you create or cherish more moments like these?

PRAYER

Dear God, thank you for the sunshine and the laughter that fills our family gatherings. May each splash and smile today remind us of your love and the bond we share.

Every ripple in the water carries the laughter and love of our family.

THE BLESSING OF A FAMILY SUMMER PRAYER

"May the Lord bless you from Zion; may you see the prosperity of Jerusalem all the days of your life. May you live to see your children's children—peace be on Israel!" **Psalm 128:5-6**

DEVOTIONAL

The joy of family is a reminder that our love and prayers have the power to shape generations.

What special moments does your family bring to mind when you think of summer prayers together? How do these shared experiences strengthen your family bonds?

PRAYER

Dear Lord, thank You for the gift of family and the time we share together in this season of warmth. May our summer prayers draw us closer to one another and to You, filling our hearts with joy and gratitude.

Together, we weave a tapestry of love
through prayer and shared moments.

AUGUST 26

THE GIFT OF A FAMILY SUMMER TRADITION

"Let us not give up meeting together, as some are in the habit of doing, but encouraging one another—and all the more as you see the Day approaching." **Hebrews 10:25**

DEVOTIONAL

The family summer tradition we hold dear not only strengthens our bond but also leaves an imprint of legacy, love, and faith for generations to come.

What are the family traditions from your own childhood that bring you joy, and how can you share them with your family this summer?

PRAYER

Dear Lord, thank You for the gift of family and the memories we create together. May our summer traditions be filled with laughter, love, and a deeper sense of togetherness.

Every tradition is a thread in the fabric of our family's story,
weaving love and connection across generations.

THE JOY OF A FAMILY SUMMER RECIPE

"Who satisfies your desires with good things so that your youth is renewed like the eagle's." Psalm 103:5

DEVOTIONAL

Cooking and sharing family recipes not only nourishes our bodies but also our hearts, reminding us that the greatest joy often comes from the simplest moments spent together.

What cherished family moments have you created in the kitchen, and how do those memories fill your heart with joy when you think of them?

PRAYER

Dear Lord, thank you for the gift of family and the joy that comes from sharing meals together. May our kitchens be filled with laughter and love as we create delicious memories with each recipe and every embrace.

Cooking together transforms ordinary
moments into extraordinary memories.

THE BLESSING OF A FAMILY SUMMER GAME

"This is the day that the Lord has made; let us rejoice and be glad in it."
Psalm 118:24

DEVOTIONAL

Cherish every moment spent in joyful play, for these are the threads that weave a family's love into an everlasting tapestry.

What does spending time with your family during a summer game mean to you, and how can you cherish those moments even more?

PRAYER

Dear Lord, thank You for the joy of family and the laughter shared in simple games. May our hearts be filled with gratitude for these precious moments spent together, weaving love and memories that last a lifetime.

Family gatherings are not just events;
they are the threads that bind our hearts together.

THE GIFT OF A FAMILY SUMMER MEMORY

"Jesus called a little child to him, and placed the child among them. He said, 'Truly I tell you, unless you change and become like little children, you will never enter the kingdom of heaven." Matthew 18:2-3

DEVOTIONAL

The most treasured memories with our families are those moments filled with laughter, story, and love; they shape our hearts and lives in ways we may not fully understand until we see the joy they bring.

What is one of your favorite summer memories with your family, and how does it continue to warm your heart today?

PRAYER

Dear Lord, thank You for the gift of family and the precious memories we share together. May each summer remind us of the laughter and love that fills our hearts. Amen.

Family memories are the threads that weave our hearts together.

FINDING JOY IN EVERYDAY MOMENTS

"Don't worry about anything; instead, pray about everything. Tell God what you need, and thank Him for all He has done. Then you will experience God's peace, which exceeds anything we can understand. His peace will guard your hearts and minds as you live in Christ Jesus." Philippians 4:6-7

DEVOTIONAL

Joy often resides in the smallest moments; take the time to cherish them and watch how they fill your heart with peace.

What small moments in your daily routine bring you joy? Can you recall a time when a simple interaction filled your heart with happiness?

PRAYER

Dear Lord, thank you for the gift of today and the simple joys that fill our lives. Help us to open our hearts to recognize and celebrate these moments, no matter how small they may seem. Amen.

Joy often hides in the gentle folds of everyday life, waiting for us to notice.

THE POWER OF A FAMILY SUMMER BLESSING

"Even to your old age and gray hairs, I am he; I am he who will sustain you. I have made you and I will carry you; I will sustain you and I will rescue you." Isaiah 46:4

DEVOTIONAL

No matter the changes life brings, the love of family is a constant blessing that reflects God's unwavering care.

What memories do you cherish most from summers spent with your family, and how can you create new blessings this year?

PRAYER

Dear Lord, thank you for the joy of family and the warmth of summer days together. Help us to embrace each moment, creating lasting memories that bind our hearts closer to You and to one another.

Summer days shared with family are the gentle threads that weave our stories together.

SEPTEMBER 1

THE BLESSING OF A NEW SEASON

"As the rain and the snow come down from heaven and do not return to it without watering the earth and making it bud and flourish, so is my word that goes out from my mouth: It will not return to me empty, but will accomplish what I desire and achieve the purpose for which I sent it."
Isaiah 55:10-11

DEVOTIONAL
Embrace each new season as a gift from God, knowing that it carries the potential for growth, love, and a cherished legacy.

What new beginnings or changes can you embrace in this season of your life to draw closer to God and your loved ones?

PRAYER
Dear Lord, thank You for the gift of new seasons in our lives. Help us to open our hearts to the blessings they bring and to trust in Your perfect timing.

Each season of life carries its own unique blessings, waiting to be discovered.

SEPTEMBER 2

THE VALUE OF HARD WORK

"In all labor there is profit, but mere talk leads only to poverty."
Proverbs 14:23

DEVOTIONAL
Labor is the bridge that connects love and devotion to those we cherish most.

What memories do you cherish from your own labor, whether in the home, your profession, or caring for loved ones? How has your hard work shaped the blessings in your life today?

PRAYER
Dear God, thank you for the beauty of hard work and the fruits it brings. Help us to appreciate the labor we have invested in our families and communities, knowing that every effort is a step toward your purpose. Amen.

Hard work is the bridge between dreams and reality.

SEPTEMBER 3

THE GIFT OF A FAMILY SCHOOL ROUTINE

"The living, the living—they praise you, as I am doing today; parents tell their children about your faithfulness." Isaiah 38:19

DEVOTIONAL

Family routines are gifts that cultivate connection, encourage faith, and nurture the hearts of loved ones.

What memories do you cherish most about your family's routines, and how have they shaped the bonds you share?

PRAYER

Dear Lord, thank you for the gift of family and the routines that draw us closer together. Help us to cherish these moments, guiding our loved ones with joy and love.

Every moment shared in routine is a thread in the fabric of family love.

SEPTEMBER 4

THE JOY OF A FAMILY FALL TRADITION

"Rejoice always, pray continually, give thanks in all circumstances; for this is God's will for you in Christ Jesus." 1 Thessalonians 5:16-18

DEVOTIONAL

Life's sweetest moments often bloom in the simplest traditions we share with our loved ones.

What is one special tradition your family shares during the fall that brings you joy and creates lasting memories together?

PRAYER

Dear Lord, thank you for the gift of family and the beautiful traditions that connect our hearts. May we cherish these moments, fostering love and joy in every gathering.

Traditions are the threads that weave our hearts together.

THE BLESSING OF A FAMILY HARVEST

"For I will contend with those who contend with you, and I will save your children." Isaiah 49:25

DEVOTIONAL

Our families are the harvest of our hearts—nurtured with love, patience, and wisdom.

What memories do you cherish most about family gatherings during harvest season, and how can you share those stories to bless the generations that follow?

PRAYER

Dear Heavenly Father, thank you for the gift of family and the abundance of love that grows in our hearts. Help us to nurture these bonds and pass down the blessings of our shared moments.

Every harvest tells a story, and every family
is a chapter in God's beautiful narrative.

SEPTEMBER 6

THE GIFT OF A FAMILY APPLE PICKING

"And Jesus said, 'Let the little children come to me, and do not hinder them, for the kingdom of God belongs to such as these." Luke 18:16

DEVOTIONAL

In the embrace of family, we find the true essence of joy; it is a reminder that love and laughter are the apples we cultivate within our lives.

What memories come to mind when you think of apple picking with your family? How do these moments reflect the love and joy that bind your family together?

PRAYER

Dear Lord, thank you for the joyful moments spent with family. Help me to cherish these times and continue to nurture the bonds we share. May our love grow deeper with each gathering.

Family is like an orchard; the more you nurture it,
the sweeter the harvest.

SEPTEMBER 7

THE POWER OF A FAMILY FALL PRAYER

"But as for me and my household, we will serve the Lord."
Exodus 20:12

DEVOTIONAL

The greatest gift we can give our families is the power of prayer, creating a bond that withstands the test of time and circumstance.

What does it mean to you to gather your family for a prayer during the fall season, and how can you encourage those moments of togetherness and gratitude?

PRAYER

Dear Lord, thank you for the gift of family and the changing seasons that remind us of your beautiful creations. May our hearts be open to share love and gratitude, both in prayer and in our daily lives together.

Together in prayer, we weave a tapestry of love
and gratitude that covers our family like a warm quilt.

SEPTEMBER 8

THE BLESSING OF A FAMILY FALL GATHERING

"But as for you, be strong and do not give up, for your work will be rewarded." **2 Chronicles 15:7**

DEVOTIONAL

The love and unity in a family gathering remind us that every moment spent together is a treasure to be cherished, for it strengthens the bonds that last a lifetime.

What are some of your fondest memories from family gatherings, and how have they shaped your understanding of love and connection over the years?

PRAYER

Dear Lord, thank You for the gift of family and the joy of gathering together. May our hearts be filled with gratitude for each precious moment shared and each story told.

Family gatherings are the threads that weave the fabric of our lives.

THE GIFT OF A FAMILY FALL PICNIC

"Therefore, if anyone is in Christ, the new creation has come: The old has gone, the new is here!" 2 Corinthians 5:17

DEVOTIONAL

Embrace every opportunity to gather your loved ones, for these moments are the threads that weave your family's story together.

What are some cherished memories you have from family gatherings, and how can you create new ones during this fall picnic?

PRAYER

Dear Lord, thank You for the gift of family and the beauty of shared moments. As we gather for this picnic, may our hearts be filled with joy and gratitude for each other.

Family is not just an important thing; it's everything.

SEPTEMBER 10

THE JOY OF A FAMILY FALL HIKE

"She speaks with wisdom, and faithful instruction is on her tongue." Proverbs 31:26

DEVOTIONAL

Every family moment, whether big or small, is a blessing to be savored and cherished.

What memories come to mind when you think of family hikes together? How do these moments bring joy and connection to your heart?

PRAYER

Dear Lord, thank you for the beauty of nature and the joy of family. May we cherish each step we take together, finding love and laughter along the way.

Every step on the trail is a step deeper into love and togetherness.

SEPTEMBER 11

PRAYING FOR PEACE

"Peace I leave with you; my peace I give you. I do not give to you as the world gives. Do not let your hearts be troubled and do not be afraid."
John 14:27

DEVOTIONAL

In times of turmoil, it is our gracious duty to instill peace in our families through prayer, gently guiding them to lean on God, who alone can mend a broken world.

What does peace mean to you in today's world, and how can you embody that peace in your daily life?

PRAYER

Dear Lord, as we gather our thoughts on this Patriot Day, we ask for Your peace to envelop our hearts and our nation. Help us to be agents of love and understanding in a world that often feels divided. Amen.

Peace begins in our hearts and flows into the lives of those around us.

SEPTEMBER 12

THE BLESSING OF A FAMILY FALL CAMPOUT

"Houses and wealth are inherited from parents, but a prudent wife is from the Lord." Proverbs 19:14

DEVOTIONAL

The blessing of family is found not in extravagant gifts, but in the simple moments shared together.

What special memories or moments do you cherish most from your family's campouts together, and how have they strengthened your bonds?

PRAYER

Dear Lord, thank you for the gift of family and the joy of creating precious memories together. Help us to cherish each moment spent in nature and with one another.

Family time in the great outdoors cultivates love, laughter, and lasting memories.

SEPTEMBER 13

THE GIFT OF A FAMILY FALL POOL DAY

"Train up a child in the way he should go; even when he is old he will not depart from it." **Proverbs 22:6**

DEVOTIONAL

Cherish the moments spent with family, for in those joyful gatherings lies the legacy of love you nurture in their hearts.

What special moments have you cherished with your family during the fall, and how can you create new memories this year as you gather by the pool?

PRAYER

Dear Lord, thank you for the blessing of family and the joy of shared moments. May our hearts be filled with gratitude as we come together, embracing laughter and love.

Family time is a tapestry woven with laughter, love, and the warmth of togetherness.

SEPTEMBER 14

THE POWER OF A FAMILY FALL TRADITION

"A good person leaves an inheritance for their children's children." **Proverbs 13:22**

DEVOTIONAL

Through our shared traditions, we weave a tapestry of love and legacy that nurtures the hearts of our family for generations to come.

What family traditions warm your heart and bring your loved ones closer together? How can you cultivate those moments to create lasting memories for generations to come?

PRAYER

Dear Lord, thank You for the gift of family and the traditions that unite us. Help us to cherish these moments and create an atmosphere of love and connection that our families can carry forward.

Traditions are the threads that weave our families together, creating a tapestry of love and memories.

SEPTEMBER 15

THE BLESSING OF A FAMILY FALL RECIPE

"Beloved, let us love one another, for love is from God; and everyone who loves is born of God and knows God." 1 John 4:7

DEVOTIONAL

Family recipes serve as a bridge, connecting generations through love, laughter, and a shared sense of belonging.

What family recipe brings back joyful memories for you? How does sharing it with your loved ones deepen your connections?

PRAYER

Dear Lord, thank you for the blessing of family and the love that is shared over meals. May our gatherings be filled with laughter, warmth, and the joy of togetherness.

Cooking is love made visible, especially when shared around the family table.

SEPTEMBER 16

THE GIFT OF A FAMILY FALL GAME

"And you will be my people, and I will be your God."
Jeremiah 30:22

DEVOTIONAL

The greatest treasures in life are not measured in material wealth, but in the joyful moments spent with family.

What is your favorite family memory from a game night, and how has it brought you closer to your loved ones over the years? Consider the joy, laughter, and sometimes playful competition that fill the air during those moments.

PRAYER

Dear God, thank you for the precious gift of family and the joy they bring into our lives. May our gatherings be filled with laughter and love, and may we cherish these moments together. Amen.

Within the simple joy of a game, we find the threads that weave our family's heart.

THE JOY OF A FAMILY FALL MEMORY

"He will renew your life and sustain you in your old age. For your daughter-in-law, who loves you and who is better to you than seven sons, has given him birth." Ruth 4:15

DEVOTIONAL
Every moment shared with family becomes a cherished memory, a reminder that love is the greatest harvest of all.

What is one cherished memory of a family fall gathering that brings a smile to your heart? How did it make you feel connected to those you love?

PRAYER
Dear Lord, thank you for the gift of family and the beautiful memories we create together, especially during the fall season. May we be reminded of your presence in these moments of joy, laughter, and love.

Family memories are the colorful leaves in the autumn of our lives, each one unique and beautiful.

THE BLESSING OF A FAMILY FALL ADVENTURE

"Since you are precious and honored in my sight, and because I love you, I will give people in exchange for you, nations in exchange for your life." Isaiah 43:4

DEVOTIONAL
Our greatest adventures can often be found in the simple joy of family gatherings, where love binds us together like the colors of autumn leaves.

What memories of family adventures do you cherish most, and how can you create new ones this fall that will bring joy to your heart?

PRAYER
Dear Lord, thank You for the blessing of family and the joy of creating memories together. Help us to appreciate each moment and to find joy in the simple adventures we share.

Life is like the changing leaves of fall—full of color, beauty, and the promise of new beginnings.

SEPTEMBER 19

THE GIFT OF A FAMILY FALL BLESSING

"Her children arise and call her blessed; her husband also,
and he praises her." Proverbs 31:28

DEVOTIONAL

Embrace each moment with your family, for the love and memories we
create are the true riches of our lives.

*What blessings has your family shared with you this fall, and how can you nurture
those connections during this season of gratitude?*

PRAYER

Dear Lord, thank you for the precious gift of family. Help us to cherish
these moments together and grow in love and understanding as the leaves
change around us.

In autumn, we gather together, not just to harvest, but to appreciate the
loved ones who shape our lives.

SEPTEMBER 20

THE POWER OF A FAMILY FALL REFLECTION

"But those who hope in the Lord will renew their strength. They will soar
on wings like eagles; they will run and not grow weary, they will walk and
not be faint." Isaiah 40:31

DEVOTIONAL

The love and stories shared among family members create a legacy that
blooms year after year.

*What moments in your life have nurtured the roots of your family tree, and how can
you gently share those stories with your loved ones this fall?*

PRAYER

Dear Lord, thank you for the gift of family. Help us to cherish the
memories of our past while creating new ones that will inspire generations
to come.

Every leaf that falls carries a story, and every family gathering is an
opportunity to weave those stories into the fabric of love.

THE BLESSING OF A FAMILY FALL GATHERING

"Be devoted to one another in love. Honor one another above yourselves."
Romans 12:10

DEVOTIONAL

The laughter and love shared at family gatherings become the heartbeats
of family memories that last a lifetime.

*What are some cherished memories you have created during family gatherings, and
how have those moments shaped your family bonds over the years?*

PRAYER

Dear Lord, thank you for the gift of family and the joy of gathering
together. May these moments be filled with love, laughter, and warmth as
we celebrate one another.

Family gatherings are the heartbeats of our lives, reminding us of love,
tradition, and the bonds that tie us together.

SEPTEMBER 22

GOD'S HARVEST

"As long as the earth endures, seedtime and harvest, cold and heat,
summer and winter, day and night will never cease." **Genesis 8:22**

DEVOTIONAL

In every season of life, may we embrace the blessings that come when we
sow love and kindness, trusting in God's perfect timing for harvest.

*What are the blessings in your life that remind you of God's bountiful harvest, and
how can you share those gifts with others this season?*

PRAYER

Dear Lord, thank you for the beauty of this season and the harvest it
brings. Help me to see and appreciate the abundance around me and to
share your love with those in my life.

Just as the leaves change and fall, so do our hearts
bear fruit in every season of life.

SEPTEMBER 23

THE GIFT OF A FAMILY FALL PICNIC

"And whatever you do, whether in word or deed, do it all in the name of the Lord Jesus, giving thanks to God the Father through Him."
Colossians 3:17

DEVOTIONAL

The greatest gift we can give our families is the time and love we share, creating memories that last a lifetime.

What special memories do you cherish from past family gatherings, and how can you create new ones during this year's picnic?

PRAYER

Dear Lord, thank You for the joy of family and the beauty of gathering together. May our hearts be filled with warmth and laughter as we celebrate the gift of our loved ones.

Family time is a precious tapestry woven with love, laughter, and shared moments.

SEPTEMBER 24

THE JOY OF A FAMILY FALL HIKE

"For you shall go out in joy and be led forth in peace; the mountains and the hills before you shall burst into song, and all the trees of the field shall clap their hands." **Isaiah 55:12**

DEVOTIONAL

The joy of family time is immeasurable, especially when shared in the beauty of nature, where laughter and love dance in the crisp autumn air.

What memories do you cherish from past family hikes, and how can you share that joy with your loved ones this fall?

PRAYER

Dear Lord, thank you for the beauty of creation and the joy of family. Help us to find peace and connection in each step we take together amidst the vibrant colors of autumn.

Each step on the trail reminds us that life's journey is best shared with those we love.

SEPTEMBER 25

THE BLESSING OF A FAMILY FALL CAMPOUT

"God sets the lonely in families."
Psalm 68:6

DEVOTIONAL
Cherish every moment spent with family, for these are the threads that stitch our hearts together in the tapestry of life.

What are some cherished memories you have of campouts with your family, and how can you pass on the joy of those experiences to your grandchildren?

PRAYER
Dear Lord, thank You for the gift of family and the memories we create together. As we gather around the campfire, may we feel Your presence in every laugh and story shared.

Family time under the stars is a reminder of the light in our lives.

SEPTEMBER 26

THE GIFT OF A FAMILY FALL POOL DAY

"She is clothed with strength and dignity;
she can laugh at the days to come." **Proverbs 31:25**

DEVOTIONAL
Every splashing laugh in the pool and joyous chatter at the table is a reminder that family fosters warmth, love, and memories that last a lifetime.

What joy does your family bring to your life, and how can you celebrate those connections in a special way today?

PRAYER
Dear Lord, thank you for the blessing of family. May our time spent together in laughter and love deepen our bonds and fill our hearts with gratitude.

Family is the anchor that holds us through life's storms.

SEPTEMBER 27

PRAYING FOR GENERATIONS TO COME

"Let your roots grow down into Him, and let your lives be built on Him.
Then your faith will grow strong in the truth you were taught, and you will
overflow with thankfulness." **Colossians 2:7**

DEVOTIONAL

Our prayers today can build a legacy of faith for the generations yet to
come.

*What dreams do you hold in your heart for the generations that will come after you?
How can your prayers today shape their paths tomorrow?*

PRAYER

Dear Lord, thank you for the gift of family and the legacy of faith. May my
prayers cover my loved ones and their future, guiding them closer to You
each day.

Your whispers of love today can echo
in the hearts of those yet to be born.

SEPTEMBER 28

THE BLESSING OF A FAMILY FALL TRADITION

"For where your treasure is, there your heart will be also."
Matthew 6:21

DEVOTIONAL

Cherish the traditions that bring your family together, for they are the
treasures that nurture love and connection.

*What family traditions do you cherish, and how do they bring joy and connection
into your home each fall?*

PRAYER

Dear Lord, thank you for the warmth of family and the cherished
traditions that knit our hearts together. May our gatherings this season be
filled with love, laughter, and gratitude for the moments we share.

Traditions are the threads that weave
our family story into a tapestry of love.

THE GIFT OF A FAMILY FALL RECIPE

"And over all these virtues put on love, which binds them all together in perfect unity." **Colossians 3:14**

DEVOTIONAL
The love seasoned in family recipes is the greatest legacy a grandmother can pass down.

What special family recipe brings back cherished memories for you, and how can you share that love with your family this fall?

PRAYER
Dear Lord, thank You for the gift of family and the memories we create around the dinner table. Help us to prepare not just meals, but love and joy in every bite we share.

Cooking together is not just about the food;
it's about nurturing relationships.

THE JOY OF A FAMILY FALL GAME

"The Lord has done great things for us, and we are filled with joy." **Psalm 126:3**

DEVOTIONAL
The simplest moments spent in joy with family can create the most cherished memories.

What memories do you cherish most about playing games with your family during the fall? How do those moments fill your heart with joy and connection?

PRAYER
Dear Lord, thank You for the laughter and love that fills our homes during family gatherings. May each game we play remind us of the bonds that unite us and the joy we share.

In the joy of play, we find the threads that weave our hearts together.

A Moment of Gratitude

If this devotional has brought moments of peace, strength, or reflection into your life, a short review on Amazon can help others discover it too.

devo.anchoredgraces.com/grandma

Even a few words about your experience can make a meaningful difference.

Thank you for continuing this journey.

OCTOBER 1

THE BLESSING OF AUTUMN COLORS

"Consider the lilies of the field, how they grow; they neither toil nor spin; yet I tell you, even Solomon in all his glory was not arrayed like one of these." Matthew 6:28-29

DEVOTIONAL

Every season holds a blessing; embrace your transforming journey and the vibrant moments shared with loved ones.

What colors of autumn resonate with your heart, and how do they remind you of the blessings in your life?

PRAYER

Dear Lord, thank You for the beautiful colors of autumn that surround us. May we find joy and gratitude in every hue as we reflect on Your goodness in our lives.

Just as the leaves change and celebrate their beauty, may we too embrace the seasons in our lives with grace.

OCTOBER 2

THE GIFT OF A FAMILY PUMPKIN PATCH

"Grandchildren are the crown of the aged, and the glory of children is their fathers." Proverbs 17:6

DEVOTIONAL

The love we cultivate in our families is like a pumpkin patch; it requires attention, care, and a willingness to nurture one another.

What memories do you cherish most about your family's time together in the pumpkin patch? How can those moments inspire you to create new traditions with your loved ones today?

PRAYER

Dear Lord, thank you for the blessings of family and the simple joys that bring us together. Help us to cherish these moments and to cultivate love and connection within our family.

Every pumpkin tells a story, and every family has a tale to share, so gather around to weave your own.

THE JOY OF A FAMILY FALL FESTIVAL

"And Jesus increased in wisdom and in stature and in favor with God and man." Luke 2:52

DEVOTIONAL

In celebrating the simple joys of life, we find the heart of family, which is the true festival of our lives.

What brings you the most joy when gathering your family together for a fall festival? How can you prepare your heart and home to create cherished memories during this special season?

PRAYER

Dear Lord, thank you for the gift of family and the joy of shared moments. May our gatherings be filled with laughter, love, and the warmth of Your presence. Bless our time together and the memories we create.

Joy blooms in the laughter of loved ones gathered, weaving memories that warm our hearts like the autumn sun.

THE BLESSING OF A FAMILY BONFIRE

"But as for me and my house, we will serve the Lord." Joshua 24:15

DEVOTIONAL

The warmth of family gatherings ignites enduring connections that remind us of the love we share.

What memories do you cherish most from family gatherings around a fire? How does the warmth of those moments light your heart today?

PRAYER

Dear Lord, thank you for the gift of family and the moments we share together. May our hearts always be drawn to one another, just like the flames that flicker and dance in our bonfire.

Family is the kindling that ignites the fire of love and laughter in our hearts.

OCTOBER 5

THE GIFT OF A FAMILY HAYRIDE

"And let us not grow weary of doing good, for in due season we will reap, if we do not give up." **Galatians 6:9**

DEVOTIONAL

In every moment we create with our families, we sow seeds of love that blossom into lasting memories.

What joyful memories do you cherish from your family hayrides, and how can those moments of connection inspire your current relationships?

PRAYER

Dear Lord, thank you for the gift of family and the laughter we share on our hayrides. May we always appreciate these simple moments that bring us closer together.

Every hayride is a reminder that love grows best when we gather together.

OCTOBER 6

THE POWER OF A FAMILY FALL BLESSING

"He who finds a wife finds what is good and receives favor from the Lord." **Proverbs 18:22**

DEVOTIONAL

Each family gathering is a seasonal blessing that nurtures our hearts and strengthens our bonds.

What does the idea of gathering your family together for a fall blessing mean to you, and how can you create a space for love and gratitude to flourish this season?

PRAYER

Dear Lord, thank You for the gift of family that surrounds us. May we cherish each moment together and share blessings that nurture our hearts.

Family is the autumn harvest of love, laughter, and lasting memories.

OCTOBER 7

THE BLESSING OF A FAMILY FALL REFLECTION

"The Lord will guide you always; he will satisfy your needs in a sun-scorched land and will strengthen your frame. You will be like a well-watered garden, like a spring whose waters never fail." Isaiah 58:11

DEVOTIONAL

Even in the fall of our lives, it is the love we nurture in our families that sustains and rejuvenates us.

What are the memories of autumn gatherings with your family that bring a smile to your heart, and how can you create new moments this season?

PRAYER

Dear Lord, thank You for the beautiful bond of family that nourishes our hearts. As we embrace the fall season, help us to cherish the moments spent together and to share the love You've bestowed upon us.

In the tapestry of life, the golden threads of family weave the warmest patterns.

OCTOBER 8

THE GIFT OF A FAMILY FALL GATHERING

"For I know the plans I have for you," declares the Lord, "plans to prosper you and not to harm you, plans to give you hope and a future."
Jeremiah 29:11

DEVOTIONAL

Family gatherings are not just about the food or the stories, but about weaving together the threads of love and memories that will be cherished for generations to come.

What is one cherished memory from a family gathering that brings you joy when you think of it? How can you create a similar moment during your next gathering?

PRAYER

Dear Lord, thank You for the blessings of family and togetherness. May our gatherings be filled with love, laughter, and shared memories, drawing us closer to one another and to You.

Family is the heart's canvas, painted with the colors of laughter, love, and cherished memories.

THE JOY OF A FAMILY FALL PICNIC

"But let all who take refuge in You rejoice; let them ever sing for joy, and spread Your protection over them, that those who love Your name may exult in You." Psalm 5:11

DEVOTIONAL

Cherish the moments spent with family, for they are the sweetest gifts that enrich our hearts and homes.

What memories and stories do you cherish most from your family gatherings, and how can you share those with your loved ones this fall?

PRAYER

Dear Lord, thank you for the gift of family that fills our hearts with love and joy. Help us to celebrate our togetherness and create lasting memories during this special season.

In the laughter of loved ones, the warmth of togetherness flourishes.

OCTOBER 10

THE BLESSING OF A FAMILY FALL HIKE

"Behold, children are a heritage from the Lord, the fruit of the womb a reward." Psalm 127:3

DEVOTIONAL

Life's greatest treasures are often found in the moments we share with our loved ones, where memories are made and bonds are strengthened.

What memories do you cherish most about spending time outdoors with your family, and how can you invite those moments into your heart during this season?

PRAYER

Dear Lord, thank You for the beauty of creation and the joy of family. Help us to savor the moments spent together, wrapped in Your presence, as we explore the wonders of the world around us.

Every step taken in nature with loved ones can deepen our bonds and nourish our spirits.

OCTOBER 11

THE GIFT OF A FAMILY FALL CAMPOUT

"Now may the God of peace Himself sanctify you completely, and may your whole spirit, soul, and body be kept blameless at the coming of our Lord Jesus Christ." 1 Thessalonians 5:23

DEVOTIONAL

Family campouts are not merely adventures; they are sacred moments where love, laughter, and life lessons are shared, creating lasting bonds that time can never erode.

What memories come to mind when you think of times spent with your family outdoors? How can you create new moments that bring joy and connection during the upcoming fall campout?

PRAYER

Dear Lord, thank You for the precious gift of family and the joy of gathering together in nature. May this fall campout be a time of laughter, connection, and cherished memories for each heart and soul present.

Family is not just an important thing;
it's everything, especially under the autumn sky.

OCTOBER 12

THE POWER OF A FAMILY FALL POOL DAY

"We love because He first loved us."
1 John 4:19

DEVOTIONAL

Cherish the moments spent together, for the love we share becomes the foundation of our most treasured memories.

What joys do you feel when you gather with your family by the pool? How do these moments strengthen the bonds that connect you all together?

PRAYER

Dear Lord, thank You for the gift of family and the laughter that fills our hearts during moments spent together. May our time in the sun and water remind us of Your love and unity.

Family is the anchor that holds us through life's storms,
offering love and joy in every splashing wave.

THE BLESSING OF A FAMILY FALL PRAYER

'For the Lord is good; His steadfast love endures forever, and His faithfulness to all generations." **Psalm 100:5**

DEVOTIONAL

Family is a living testament of God's enduring love, a blessing to be cherished and nurtured through prayer and gratitude.

What moments this fall remind you of the blessings
your family brings into your life?

PRAYER

Dear Lord, thank you for the gift of family. As the autumn leaves fall, may we embrace the warmth of each other's love and support. Help us to cherish these moments together.

In the gentle rustle of leaves lies the sound of family laughter, a reminder of love that nurtures our souls.

OCTOBER 14

EXPLORING NEW PATHS

"See, I am doing a new thing! Now it springs up; do you not perceive it? I am making a way in the wilderness and streams in the wasteland." **Isaiah 43:19**

DEVOTIONAL

Embracing new opportunities, even in small ways, can lead to enriching experiences that expand our hearts and lives.

What new paths are you being invited to explore in this season of your life, and how
can you open your heart to embrace them?

PRAYER

Dear Lord, help me to lean into the changes and new adventures that come my way. Grant me the courage to step forward with joy and the wisdom to see Your guiding hand in each step I take. Amen.

Growth often lies just beyond the comfort of familiarity.

OCTOBER 15

THE GIFT OF A FAMILY FALL TRADITION

"Therefore encourage one another and build each other up, just as in fact you are doing." 1 Thessalonians 5:11

DEVOTIONAL

Family traditions, no matter how simple, create lasting bonds that turn moments into cherished memories.

What is one special tradition in your family that brings everyone together during the fall season, and how can you nurture that bond this year?

PRAYER

Dear Lord, thank you for the beauty of family traditions that draw us closer. Help us to cherish these moments and create new memories filled with love and laughter.

Tradition is the warmth that wraps around us,
binding generations together.

OCTOBER 16

THE JOY OF A FAMILY FALL RECIPE

"Until now you have asked nothing in my name. Ask, and you will receive, that your joy may be full." John 16:24

DEVOTIONAL

In every recipe shared, there are ingredients of love and connection that nourish the soul.

What is a special recipe that brings your family together during the fall season, and what memories do you associate with preparing and sharing it?

PRAYER

Dear God, thank you for the joy of family and the warmth that sharing meals brings. May the love and laughter around our tables nourish our hearts and strengthen our bonds.

Cooking together is not just about making food; it's about creating cherished moments that fill our hearts with joy.

OCTOBER 17

THE BLESSING OF A FAMILY FALL GAME

"To provide for those who grieve in Zion—to bestow on them a crown of beauty instead of ashes, the oil of joy instead of mourning, and a garment of praise instead of a spirit of despair. They will be called oaks of righteousness, a planting of the Lord for the display of his splendor."
Isaiah 61:3

DEVOTIONAL

Cherish the joy that comes from gathering your family, for in those moments, you weave a tapestry of love and memories that bless generations.

What memories flood your heart when you think of your family gathered together for fun and laughter during fall game nights? How can you create even more cherished moments this season?

PRAYER

Dear Lord, thank You for the blessing of family and the joy that games can bring. May our hearts be filled with love as we gather, sharing laughter and memories that will last a lifetime.

Every touch of laughter during a family game night
weaves the fabric of our love even tighter.

OCTOBER 18

THE GIFT OF A FAMILY FALL MEMORY

"Lord, you alone are my portion and my cup; you make my lot secure. The boundary lines have fallen for me in pleasant places; surely I have a delightful inheritance." Psalm 16:5-6

DEVOTIONAL

The memories we create with our families in the simple moments of togetherness are treasures that can warm our hearts for a lifetime.

What treasured memories have you gathered with your family during the fall? Can you recall the laughter, the shared meals, or perhaps a cozy evening spent together, wrapped in blankets while watching the leaves fall?

PRAYER

Dear Lord, thank You for the gift of family, especially during this beautiful season. May we always cherish the moments spent with loved ones, creating memories that warm our hearts and inspire joy.

Every moment shared is a thread woven into the fabric of our lives.

THE POWER OF A FAMILY FALL ADVENTURE

"One generation commends your works to another; they tell of your mighty acts." **Psalm 145:4**

DEVOTIONAL

Each autumn adventure with family is a beautiful reminder of the love we have to share that weaves generations together.

What family fall memory warms your heart the most, and how can you create new ones with your loved ones this season?

PRAYER

Dear Lord, thank you for the gift of family and the precious memories we share. Help us to cherish these moments and create new ones that will last a lifetime.

Each leaf that falls is a story, each gathering a memory— woven together, they create the tapestry of our lives.

OCTOBER 20

THE BLESSING OF A FAMILY FALL BLESSING

"Listen, my son, to your father's instruction and do not forsake your mother's teaching. They are a garland of grace to your head and a chain to adorn your neck." **Proverbs 1:8-9**

DEVOTIONAL

Family is a precious heritage, and the teachings we pass down are gifts that bless generations.

What special moments do you cherish with your family during the fall season, and how can you create new traditions that celebrate these blessings?

PRAYER

Dear Lord, thank you for the gift of family and the joy of gathering together. May our hearts be filled with gratitude as we celebrate each precious moment and create lasting memories this fall.

Family is the harvest of love, and each shared moment is a golden leaf in our heart's collection.

OCTOBER 21

THE GIFT OF A FAMILY FALL REFLECTION

"All your children shall be taught by the Lord, and great shall be the peace of your children." Isaiah 54:13

DEVOTIONAL

No matter the challenges, the love and faith you share with your family create lasting peace that embraces each generation.

What memories do the changing colors of fall bring to your heart, and how has your family shaped those moments over the years?

PRAYER

Dear Lord, thank You for the wonderful gift of family. May we cherish every moment together, remembering the joy that each season brings into our lives.

Family is the warm blanket that wraps around us, especially in life's changing seasons.

OCTOBER 22

THE JOY OF A FAMILY FALL GATHERING

"He tends His flock like a shepherd: He gathers the lambs in His arms and carries them close to His heart." Isaiah 40:11

DEVOTIONAL

In the tapestry of life, it is these colorful threads of family and togetherness that weave the most beautiful patterns in our hearts.

What special memories does your family gathering bring to mind, and how can you create new moments of joy together this fall?

PRAYER

Dear Lord, thank You for the gift of family and the joy that fills our hearts during our gatherings. May each shared moment be filled with love and laughter, drawing us closer to one another and to You.

Gathering together is a reminder that love is a thread that binds generations.

OCTOBER 23

THE BLESSING OF A FAMILY FALL PICNIC

"The righteous man walks in his integrity; his children are blessed after him." **Proverbs 20:7**

DEVOTIONAL

Cherishing moments like these reminds us of the importance of nurturing family bonds, creating memories that last a lifetime, and instilling love and faith through our actions.

What favorite memory do you hold close from past family gatherings that you wish to recreate at this year's fall picnic?

PRAYER

Dear Lord, thank you for the beautiful blessing of family. May this picnic be a time of love, laughter, and connection as we gather around the warmth of each other's hearts.

Gathering together in nature's embrace ignites the bond of love that weaves our family closer.

OCTOBER 24

THE GIFT OF A FAMILY FALL HIKE

"O Lord, what a variety of things you have made! In wisdom, you have made them all. The earth is full of your creatures; there is the ocean, vast and wide, teeming with life of every kind, both small and large." **Psalm 104:24-25**

DEVOTIONAL

Life's most precious moments often unfold in the beauty of nature, reminding us of the love and connection we share within our families.

What are the special moments you cherish with your family during the changing seasons, and how do they remind you of God's blessings in your life?

PRAYER

Dear Lord, thank you for the gift of family and the beauty of nature. Help us to cherish each moment we share together, finding joy in the simple pleasures of life.

Embrace each step taken in love, for in those moments, we discover the true essence of family.

OCTOBER 25

THE POWER OF A FAMILY FALL CAMPOUT

"...consider how we may spur one another on toward love and good deeds, not giving up meeting together." Hebrews 10:24-25

DEVOTIONAL

Cherish the peaceful moments with family, for they are the roots that nourish the heart.

What memories does your family campout evoke? How do those shared moments shape the love and bond within your family today? Consider the joy, the laughter, and perhaps even the lessons learned during those times spent around the campfire.

PRAYER

Dear Lord, thank you for the gift of family and the memories we create together. May our moments spent in nature remind us of Your love and the beauty of connection. Amen.

Family time in the great outdoors weaves a tapestry of love and memories that last a lifetime.

OCTOBER 26

THE BLESSING OF A FAMILY FALL POOL DAY

"And these words that I command you today shall be on your heart. You shall teach them diligently to your children and shall talk of them when you sit in your house, and when you walk by the way, and when you lie down, and when you rise." Deuteronomy 6:6-7

DEVOTIONAL

Every moment spent with family is an opportunity to share love, laughter, and life lessons that will echo in their hearts for generations.

What are some cherished memories you hold from family gatherings, and how can you create new ones during your next pool day?

PRAYER

Dear Lord, thank You for the joy of family gatherings. May each splash and laughter echo the love we share, bringing us closer together as we create memories that last a lifetime.

In the gentle ripples of the pool, we find the joy that binds our hearts together.

THE GIFT OF A FAMILY FALL PRAYER

"How can we thank God enough for you in return for all the joy we have in the presence of our God because of you?" 1 Thessalonians 3:9

DEVOTIONAL

Every family season brings blessings to cherish and lessons to learn; each moment together is a reminder of God's love manifesting in our lives.

What does your heart hold when you think of your family gathering together this fall?

PRAYER

Dear God, thank you for the beautiful gift of family.
May our hearts be filled with love, and may our shared moments be blessed with warmth and peace.

In the embrace of family, we find the warmth of love
and the strength of togetherness.

OCTOBER 28

THE JOY OF A FAMILY FALL TRADITION

"Fear not, for I am with you; be not dismayed, for I am your God; I will strengthen you, I will help you, I will uphold you with my righteous right hand." Isaiah 41:10

DEVOTIONAL

Let the joy of family traditions remind you that these moments are treasures that enrich our hearts and souls.

What fall traditions does your family cherish, and how do they bring you closer together? Think about the laughter shared, the stories told, and the love that deepens with each autumn gathering.

PRAYER

Dear Lord, thank You for the gift of family and the traditions that bind us together. May every moment shared this fall fill our hearts with joy and gratitude, reminding us of Your love.

Family traditions are the threads that weave our hearts
into a tapestry of love and memories.

OCTOBER 29

THE BLESSING OF A FAMILY FALL RECIPE

"Every good and perfect gift is from above, coming down from the Father of the heavenly lights. He does not change like shifting shadows." James 1:17

DEVOTIONAL

The true blessing of family lies not only in the recipes we share but in the love and connections that flourish in our homes.

What cherished family recipe brings back the sweetest memories for you? How can you use that recipe to create new moments with your loved ones this fall?

PRAYER

Dear God, thank You for the love that knits our families together. May we find joy in sharing meals and moments, nurturing bonds that last a lifetime.

Love is the secret ingredient in every family recipe.

OCTOBER 30

THE GIFT OF A FAMILY FALL GAME

"If you then, who are evil, know how to give good gifts to your children, how much more will your Father who is in heaven give good things to those who ask him!" Matthew 7:11

DEVOTIONAL

Family moments are the priceless gifts that enrich our lives and create lasting legacies

What memories does your family's fall gathering bring to mind, and how can you cherish or strengthen those bonds during your next game together?

PRAYER

Dear Lord, thank you for the gift of family and the joy that comes from shared laughter and memories. May our time spent together in games and fun deepen our love and connection.

Family time becomes a treasure chest of laughter, moments, and love, especially during joyful gatherings.

LIGHT IN THE DARKNESS

"You are the light of the world. A town built on a hill cannot be hidden. Neither do people light a lamp and put it under a bowl. Instead, they put it on its stand, and it gives light to everyone in the house." Matthew 5:14-16

DEVOTIONAL

Let your light shine brightly, even in the shadowy corners of the world, for your love and wisdom can be a guiding star to those who may feel lost.

What does 'light in the darkness' mean to you personally, especially in a world that often seems filled with shadows and uncertainty?

PRAYER

Dear Lord, thank you for being our guiding light through every season of life. Help us to shine Your love in the dark corners of our world this Halloween and beyond.

When we are anchored in the light, even the darkest nights can become a time of hope and renewal.

NOVEMBER 1

REMEMBERING FAITHFUL LIVES

"Blessed are those whose strength is in You, who have set their hearts on pilgrimage. As they pass through the Valley of Baca, they make it a place of springs; the autumn rains also cover it with pools." **Psalm 84:5-6**

DEVOTIONAL

In remembering the faithful lives of others, we deepen our own faith and understand that we, too, are part of a larger narrative filled with hope, love, and perseverance.

What moments from your life remind you of the faithful women who have influenced your journey? How can their stories inspire you to share your own faith with those around you?

PRAYER

Dear Lord, thank you for the faithful women in our lives who have shaped our faith. May we honor their legacy by sharing love and wisdom with others, just as they did for us.

Every moment spent in faith is a thread
woven into the tapestry of our lives.

NOVEMBER 2

THE BLESSING OF A FAMILY THANKSGIVING PREP

"The wise woman builds her house, but with her own hands, the foolish one tears hers down." **Proverbs 14:1**

DEVOTIONAL

In every shared meal prepped with love, we weave the fabric of our family's heritage and strengthen our bonds.

What special memories come to mind when you think of family gatherings and the joy of preparing for Thanksgiving together? How does your heart feel when you remember those moments?

PRAYER

Dear Lord, thank You for the blessing of family and the joy of gathering around the table. May our hearts be filled with gratitude as we prepare, creating memories that will last a lifetime.

Thanksgiving is not just a day, but a spirit of gratitude
woven into the fabric of family love.

THE GIFT OF A FAMILY GRATITUDE JOURNAL

"In everything give thanks; for this is the will of God in Christ Jesus for you." 1 Thessalonians 5:18

DEVOTIONAL

Gratitude has a transformative power that can deepen family bonds and lift our spirits, reminding us to cherish the joys that each day brings.

What moments of gratitude have touched your heart recently, and how can you invite your family to share in those blessings with you?

PRAYER

Heavenly Father, thank you for the gift of family and the love that binds us together. Help us to find joy in sharing our gratitude with one another, creating memories that last a lifetime.

Gratitude shared is love multiplied.

NOVEMBER 4

THE JOY OF A FAMILY HARVEST

"Those who sow in tears will reap with songs of joy. He who goes out weeping, carrying seed to sow, will return with songs of joy, carrying sheaves with him." Psalm 126:5-6

DEVOTIONAL

The joy of a family harvest comes not only from the fruits we gather but also from the love and care we invest along the way.

What are some ways you can actively celebrate the unique blessings your family brings into your life?

PRAYER

Dear Lord, thank you for the beautiful harvest of love and memories that my family brings. Help me to cherish each moment and to find joy in the simple acts of togetherness.

Every smile shared around the family table is a thread woven into the tapestry of love.

EMBRACING CHANGE WITH GRACE

"Forget the former things; do not dwell on the past. See, I am doing a new thing! Now it springs up; do you not perceive it? I am making a way in the wilderness and streams in the wasteland." Isaiah 43:18-19

DEVOTIONAL

Embracing change allows us to recognize the beauty in new beginnings and the bonds that grow stronger through life's transitions.

What changes have you faced recently, and how can you open your heart to embrace them with grace and gratitude?

PRAYER

Dear God, thank you for the gift of each new day. Help me to see the beauty in change and to trust in your plans for my life.

Embracing change is not about losing what we love; it's about finding new ways to love what remains.

CHERISHING MULTIGENERATIONAL BONDS

"Instead, we were like young children among you. Just as a nursing mother cares for her children, so we cared for you. Because we loved you so much, we were delighted to share with you not only the gospel of God but our lives as well." 1 Thessalonians 2:7-8

DEVOTIONAL

The love and connection we nurture with our family create lasting legacies that enrich our lives and the lives of those who follow.

What are some cherished moments you've shared with your grandchildren that have strengthened your bond?

PRAYER

Dear Lord, thank You for the gift of family. Help us to nurture our relationships across generations and to celebrate the love that binds us together.

Each moment spent with family is a treasure that grows richer with time.

NOVEMBER 7

INTERCEDING FOR LOVED ONES

"And pray in the Spirit on all occasions with all kinds of prayers and requests." **Ephesians 6:18a**

DEVOTIONAL

Every prayer we offer for our loved ones is a gift woven into the fabric of their lives, bringing them closer to God's grace.

What loved one is on your heart today, and how might God be inviting you to pray for them in a deeper way? Consider the specific challenges they face and the joys they might need encouragement in. How can your faith uplift them?

PRAYER

Dear Lord, thank you for the gift of family and friends. I ask for your grace to cover my loved ones today, bringing them strength, peace, and hope in their challenges. Amen.

Through our prayers, we become the gentle lifeline lifting our loved ones toward Heaven.

NOVEMBER 8

CREATING NEW TRADITIONS WITH GRANDCHILDREN

"This is my commandment, that you love one another as I have loved you." **John 15:12**

DEVOTIONAL

Traditions don't just carry the past; they also create beautiful moments in the present.

What new traditions could you create with your grandchildren that would bring joy and strengthen your bond? Have you thought about what memories you would like to share together?

PRAYER

Dear God, thank you for the gift of family. Please help me to create special moments with my grandchildren that will last a lifetime. Amen.

Traditions weave the fabric of our family's love.

PASSING DOWN SECRET FAMILY RECIPES

"Stand up in the presence of the elderly, and show respect for the aged."
Leviticus 19:32

DEVOTIONAL

Our family recipes are not just about nourishment; they are a legacy of love and tradition that we pass on with every meal shared.

What cherished recipes have been passed down in your family, and how do they connect you to your loved ones?

PRAYER

Dear God, thank you for the gift of family and the love expressed through our recipes. May our kitchens be filled with laughter and the warmth of shared memories as we pass down our traditions.

Every recipe tells a story; each dish is a thread
that weaves our family tapestry together.

NOVEMBER 10

THE GIFT OF TOGETHERNESS

"A glad heart makes a cheerful face,
but by sorrow of heart the spirit is crushed." **Proverbs 15:13**

DEVOTIONAL

The greatest gift we can give ourselves and our families is the time spent together, where love flourishes and hearts connect deeply.

What are some cherished memories you hold that highlight the beauty of togetherness with your loved ones? How can you cultivate more moments like these in your life today?

PRAYER

Dear Lord, thank you for the gift of family and friends. Help us to cherish our moments together and to find joy in every shared laughter and conversation.

Togetherness is the thread that weaves our hearts
into a beautiful tapestry of love.

NOVEMBER 11

HONORING SERVICE

"Greater love has no one than this: to lay down one's life for one's friends."
John 15:13

DEVOTIONAL
Cherish the stories of sacrifice and service, for they are treasures that shape our understanding of love and freedom.

What memories come to your mind when you think of the veterans in your life, and how can you honor their sacrifices today?

PRAYER
Dear Lord, we thank You for the brave men and women who have served our country. Help us to honor their sacrifice with our words and deeds, reflecting Your love and grace in our gratitude.

True strength lies in the willingness to serve others.

NOVEMBER 12

THE BLESSING OF A FAMILY FALL MEMORY

"Your wife will be like a fruitful vine within your house; your children will be like olive shoots around your table." Psalm 128:3

DEVOTIONAL
Family memories are the blessings that nurture our hearts and strengthen our roots.

What cherished family memory from this fall brings a smile to your heart? How can you pass on that joy to the next generation?

PRAYER
Dear Lord, thank You for the precious moments we share with our families. May we continue to create and cherish memories that honor love and togetherness.

Family memories are the petals of our hearts,
each one holding a story of love and laughter.

THE GIFT OF A FAMILY FALL ADVENTURE

"And above all these put on love, which binds everything together in perfect harmony." Colossians 3:14

DEVOTIONAL

The joy of family time is not found in the extravagant but in the little things—let your heart be open to create cherished memories with those you love.

What special memories have you created with your family during fall adventures in the past, and how can you inspire new ones this season?

PRAYER

Dear Lord, thank You for the gift of family and the joy that shared moments bring. Help us to cherish each adventure, big or small, as we create lasting memories together.

Every autumn adventure with family is a thread woven into the fabric of our shared story.

NOVEMBER 14

SPEAKING WORDS OF BLESSING OVER LOVED ONES

"The tongue has the power of life and death, and those who love it will eat its fruit." Proverbs 18:21

DEVOTIONAL

Speak words of blessing over your loved ones daily, for your encouragement can plant seeds of love that flourish through seasons of life.

What words of blessing can you speak over your loved ones today to uplift their spirits and encourage their hearts?

PRAYER

Dear God, thank you for the gift of family. Help us to recognize the power of our words, and may they always reflect Your love and grace as we speak blessings over those we cherish.

Your words have the power to shape the world around you; let them be filled with love and kindness.

NOVEMBER 15

FINDING BEAUTY IN AUTUMN'S CHANGES

"And why do you worry about clothes? See how the flowers of the field grow. They do not labor or spin. Yet I tell you that not even Solomon in all his splendor was dressed like one of these." **Matthew 6:28-29**

DEVOTIONAL

As you embrace the richness of this season, remember that change is not to be feared but celebrated, for it often leads us to a more beautiful path ahead.

What changes in your life have brought you unexpected beauty this autumn? Can you see the blessings in the transition around you?

PRAYER

Dear God, thank you for the beauty of this season and the wisdom that comes with change. Help us embrace the transformations in our lives, trusting that each one brings us closer to Your love and grace.

Autumn teaches us that change can be beautiful,
and sometimes the most colorful lessons come from letting go.

NOVEMBER 16

SHARING STORIES AROUND THE TABLE

"And they shall be as a tree planted by the rivers of water, that bringeth forth his fruit in his season." **Psalm 1:3**

DEVOTIONAL

Every story you share is like a seed planted in the hearts of your loved ones, growing into understanding and wisdom.

What stories from your own life do you cherish the most, and how can sharing them around the table strengthen your family's bonds today?

PRAYER

Dear Lord, thank You for the gift of family and the wisdom of shared stories. May our conversations around the table be filled with love, laughter, and the richness of our experiences.

Every story shared is a thread woven into the fabric of our family,
connecting us across generations.

NOVEMBER 17

SAVORING GOD'S CREATION OUTDOORS

"For since the creation of the world God's invisible qualities—his eternal power and divine nature—have been clearly seen, being understood from what has been made, so that people are without excuse." Romans 1:20

DEVOTIONAL

Every time we step outside, we have an opportunity to connect with God through His wondrous creation, finding beauty in the details and peace for our hearts.

What does the beauty of a flower or the song of a bird reveal to you about God's love for creation and for you?

PRAYER

Dear Lord, thank You for the gift of nature and for the moments spent in Your beautiful creation. Help us to slow down and truly savor the wonders You have placed around us.

To walk among the flowers is to walk in the presence of the Creator.

NOVEMBER 18

WALKING IN GOD'S PRESENCE

"You make known to me the path of life; in your presence there is fullness of joy; at your right hand are pleasures forevermore." Psalm 16:11

DEVOTIONAL

We can find God in the simple moments of our days, reminding us that His presence brings joy and peace.

What does it mean for you to consciously walk in God's presence each day, and how can you cultivate this awareness in your life?

PRAYER

Dear Heavenly Father, thank You for the gift of Your constant presence. Help us to feel Your love surrounding us in every moment and guide us to share that love with those around us.

Walking in God's presence turns ordinary moments into sacred encounters.

FINDING PEACE UNDER THE STARS

"Come to me, all you who are weary and burdened, and I will give you rest. Take my yoke upon you and learn from me, for I am gentle and humble in heart, and you will find rest for your souls." Matthew 11:28-29

DEVOTIONAL

Let the night sky remind you that, in moments of worry, seeking God's presence under the stars will always bring you peace.

What does it mean for you to find peace in your life, especially during times of uncertainty? Can you recall a moment when the vastness of the night sky brought you comfort or clarity?

PRAYER

Dear Lord, thank You for the beauty of the night sky that reminds us of Your greatness and love. Help us to rest in Your peace, even when the world feels overwhelming. May we find solace in Your presence tonight.

Just as the stars shine their brightest in the darkest of skies, so too can our hearts radiate peace amidst life's storms.

NOVEMBER 20

REFRESHING OUR SPIRITS

"We have this hope as an anchor for the soul, firm and secure."
Hebrews 6:19

DEVOTIONAL

Take time to refresh your spirit through acts of love and kindness, like watering a flower, for in caring for others, you too will bloom anew.

What are the little joys in your life that can help rejuvenate your spirit today?

PRAYER

Dear Lord, thank You for the gift of this day. May Your love fill our hearts and bring us peace as we seek moments of refreshment in our lives.

Just as a garden flourishes with care, our spirits bloom
when nurtured with love and attention.

TRUSTING GOD WITH FAMILY CONCERNS

"Cast all your anxiety on him because he cares for you."
1 Peter 5:7

DEVOTIONAL

Trusting God allows us to let go of our worries and embrace His love for our family.

What family concerns are weighing on your heart today, and how can you lean into God's presence to find peace and clarity?

PRAYER

Dear Heavenly Father, thank you for the gift of family. Help me to trust you with my loved ones and guide me in the ways I can support them best.

Trusting God opens the door to His peace, even amid family storms.

NOVEMBER 22

HONORING THE PAST, EMBRACING THE FUTURE

"Gray hair is a crown of splendor; it is attained by a righteous life."
Proverbs 16:31

DEVOTIONAL

Remember that honoring your past not only shapes who you are but also enriches the future generations who look up to you.

What are some precious memories from your past that still bring you joy, and how can they inspire you as you look forward to new experiences in the years to come?

PRAYER

Dear Lord, thank you for the gift of our past and the promise of our future. Help us to cherish our memories while courageously stepping into the days ahead with hope and grace.

Every chapter of our lives holds lessons and love
that shape who we are becoming.

COOKING WITH LOVE FOR THE NEXT GENERATION

"Let everything you do be done in love."
1 Corinthians 16:14

DEVOTIONAL

Cooking is not simply a task; it is a way to share love and heritage, creating moments that become treasured memories for the next generation.

What are some of your favorite recipes that have been passed down in your family, and how do you hope to share those traditions with your grandchildren?

PRAYER

Dear Lord, as I gather ingredients to create meals for my family, may each dish be filled with love and the warmth of cherished memories. Help me to pass on not just recipes, but the joy and connection that come from cooking together. Amen.

Cooking with love turns ordinary meals into cherished memories.

NOVEMBER 24

THANKSGIVING: GRATEFUL HEARTS

"Enter His gates with thanksgiving and His courts with praise; give thanks to Him and praise His name. For the Lord is good and His love endures forever; His faithfulness continues through all generations." **Psalm 100:4-5**

DEVOTIONAL

Gratitude opens our eyes to the beauty around us and teaches us to cherish even the simplest moments.

What are the little things in your daily life that fill your heart with gratitude, and how can you express this thankfulness to those around you?

PRAYER

Dear Lord, thank you for the gifts of family, friendships, and the beauty of each day. Help us to cultivate a spirit of gratitude that reflects Your love and kindness.

Gratitude turns what we have into enough.

GIVING THANKS IN ALL SEASONS

"In everything give thanks; for this is the will of God in Christ Jesus concerning you." 1 Thessalonians 5:18

DEVOTIONAL

Remember, dear ones, that cultivating a grateful heart brings joy and peace, no matter the season of life you find yourself in.

How can you cultivate a heart of gratitude in both joy and hardship? What small moments today can you cherish and bring before God in thankfulness?

PRAYER

Dear Lord, thank You for the gift of every day. Help us to see Your blessings in the little moments and to have hearts overflowing with gratitude, no matter the season we find ourselves in.

In every season, there is a reason to give thanks.

THE GIFT OF A FAMILY THANKSGIVING MEAL

"And let the peace of Christ rule in your hearts, to which indeed you were called in one body. And be thankful." Colossians 3:15

DEVOTIONAL

Family is a precious gift, and the time spent together, especially over a meal, is a sacred sharing of love and thankfulness.

What special memories do you cherish from past Thanksgiving meals with your family, and how can you create new ones this year?

PRAYER

Dear Lord, as we gather around the table with our loved ones, may our hearts be filled with gratitude. Help us to appreciate each moment and the gift of family.

Thanksgiving is not just a meal;
it's the gathering of hearts and stories around the table.

THE POWER OF A FAMILY THANKSGIVING PRAYER

"Let us come before Him with thanksgiving and extol Him
with music and song." **Psalm 95:2**

DEVOTIONAL

The simple act of offering a thanksgiving prayer can strengthen families
and create lasting memories of love and gratitude.

*What does Thanksgiving mean to you as you gather with your loved ones, and how
can you express gratitude in your family's prayer this year?*

PRAYER

Dear Lord, thank you for the gift of family and the love we share. As we
come together in gratitude, may our hearts be filled with joy and
thankfulness for each moment spent together.

Family prayer binds our hearts and nurtures our souls.

PRACTICING HOSPITALITY WITH A JOYFUL HEART

"Offer hospitality to one another without grumbling."
1 Peter 4:9

DEVOTIONAL

When we open our homes and hearts with joy, we create spaces where love
and connection flourish.

*What brings you joy when you welcome others into your home? How can you create
an even warmer space for your loved ones to feel cherished and valued?*

PRAYER

Dear Lord, thank You for the gift of hospitality and the joy it brings. Help
me to open my heart and home to others, reflecting Your love in every
gathering.

Hospitality is not just about inviting others in,
but about embracing them in love.

NOVEMBER 29

THE GIFT OF A FAMILY THANKSGIVING TRADITION

"Honor your father and mother, which is the first commandment with a promise." Ephesians 6:2

DEVOTIONAL

Family traditions, like Thanksgiving gatherings, can become the threads that weave our family together, reminding us of the importance of honoring our roots while nurturing new branches.

What memories do you cherish most from your family's Thanksgiving gatherings, and how can you nurture those traditions for the younger generations?

PRAYER

Dear Lord, thank you for the blessings of family and the warmth of togetherness. Help us to cultivate traditions that bring joy and connection for years to come.

Traditions are the threads that weave our family's story together.

NOVEMBER 30

THE JOY OF A FAMILY THANKSGIVING REFLECTION

"The name of the Lord is a strong tower; the righteous run to it and are safe." Proverbs 18:10

DEVOTIONAL

This Thanksgiving, let us cherish each moment, recognizing that our time together is a gift not to be taken for granted. The laughter, stories, and shared memories weave the fabric of our family's legacy, and it's in these sacred times that we nurture our connections.

What moments during this Thanksgiving have brought you the deepest sense of joy and connection with your family? Can you recall a particular memory or story that filled your heart with gratitude?

PRAYER

Dear Lord, thank You for the blessing of family and the joy they bring to our lives. Help us to cherish these moments together and to continue creating loving memories. Amen.

Thanksgiving is a tapestry woven with
love, laughter, and cherished memories.

DECEMBER 1

WAITING WITH HOPE

"Do not let your hearts be troubled. Trust in God; trust also in me. In my Father's house are many rooms; if it were not so, I would have told you. I am going there to prepare a place for you." John 14:1-3

DEVOTIONAL

Waiting with hope helps us cherish the moments we have now, nurturing our hearts and the hearts of others.

What does waiting with hope mean to you in this season of Advent, and how can you embrace the moments of stillness with expectation? Think of a time when hope filled your heart—how might that experience influence your waiting now?

PRAYER

Dear Lord, as I journey through this season of Advent, help me to embrace the gift of waiting. May my heart be filled with hope, preparing for the joy of your coming. Amen.

Hope is the gentle thread that weaves through our waiting, binding our hearts to the promises yet to unfold.

DECEMBER 2

THE BLESSING OF A FAMILY CHRISTMAS PREP

"She is clothed with strength and dignity; she can laugh at the days to come." Proverbs 31:25

DEVOTIONAL

Amid the hustle and bustle of family Christmas preparations, treasure the moments of togetherness that bless your heart and weave your family's fabric even tighter.

What are some cherished memories you have of preparing for Christmas with your family, and how do you hope to create new ones this year?

PRAYER

Dear Lord, thank You for the gift of family and the joy of preparing together for this special season. May our hearts be filled with love and our homes with laughter as we celebrate the true meaning of Christmas.

Christmas is not just a season; it's a tapestry woven with love, laughter, and shared moments.

DECEMBER 3

THE GIFT OF A FAMILY CHRISTMAS TREE

"For to us a child is born, to us a son is given..."
Isaiah 9:6

DEVOTIONAL

Every ornament on your tree is a reminder that the love of family shines brightest during the holidays.

What memories does your family Christmas tree hold for you? As you decorate it, how does each ornament remind you of the love and joy shared over the years?

PRAYER

Dear Lord, thank you for the warmth of family during this Christmas season. May each ornament we hang on our tree fill our hearts with gratitude for the memories and love they represent.

A family Christmas tree is more than just decorations; it is a tapestry of love, laughter, and togetherness woven through the years.

DECEMBER 4

THE JOY OF A FAMILY CHRISTMAS TRADITION

"And do not forget to do good and to share with others, for with such sacrifices God is pleased." Hebrews 13:16

DEVOTIONAL

As we celebrate our family traditions, let us remember that it's the shared moments and memories that bring immeasurable joy and fortify the bonds we hold dear.

What is one special Christmas tradition in your family that brings you joy and connects you to your loved ones? How has it shaped your family's appreciation for this special season?

PRAYER

Dear Lord, thank You for the gift of family and the traditions that bind our hearts together. As we celebrate this Christmas season, help us to cherish the moments that bring us joy and connect us deeper with those we love.

Traditions are the threads that weave our family together, creating a tapestry of love and memory.

DECEMBER 5

THE BLESSING OF A FAMILY CHRISTMAS RECIPE

"But the fruit of the Spirit is love, joy, peace, forbearance, kindness, goodness, faithfulness, gentleness, and self-control. Against such things there is no law." Galatians 5:22-23

DEVOTIONAL

Treasure the moments spent with family as they become the sweetest memories that fill your heart for a lifetime.

What cherished recipe brings your family together each Christmas, and what memories swirl around it that make it special for you?

PRAYER

Dear Lord, thank you for the gift of family and the joy that comes from sharing meals together. Bless our homes this Christmas season with laughter and warmth as we gather around our favorite dishes.

Every bite of a cherished recipe carries the love
and stories of those who've shared it.

DECEMBER 6

THE GIFT OF A FAMILY CHRISTMAS CARD

"For where your treasure is, there your heart will be also."
Luke 12:34

DEVOTIONAL

Creating a simple family Christmas card can become a treasured reminder of love and connection for generations to come.

What memories flood your heart when you think about the family Christmas cards you've received over the years? How do these cards remind you of the love and connections that bind your family together?

PRAYER

Dear Lord, thank You for the gift of family and the joy that Christmas brings. Help us to cherish each moment together and hold dear the love we share, as we celebrate this special season.

Each card tells a story, a snapshot of love that warms the heart.

THE POWER OF A FAMILY CHRISTMAS PRAYER

"Therefore, as God's chosen people, holy and dearly loved, clothe yourselves with compassion, kindness, humility, gentleness and patience."
Colossians 3:12

DEVOTIONAL

The power of a family Christmas prayer creates a sacred space where love, gratitude, and hope flourish together.

What memory do you cherish most about family gatherings during the Christmas season, and how can prayer deepen those connections this year?

PRAYER

Dear Lord, thank you for the gift of family and the love that binds us together. As we gather this Christmas, may our hearts be open to your presence, and may our prayers bring us closer to one another and to you.

Prayer, like a warm blanket, wraps us in love
and connection, no matter the distance.

DECEMBER 8

THE BLESSING OF A FAMILY CHRISTMAS MEMORY

"May the Lord bless you from Zion; may you see the prosperity of Jerusalem all the days of your life. May you live to see your children's children—peace be on Israel!" **Psalm 128:5-6**

DEVOTIONAL

The best gifts do not come neatly wrapped, but are instead the memories we create together as a family, shared in love and laughter.

What cherished family tradition do you hold dear that brings a smile to your heart each Christmas?

PRAYER

Dear Heavenly Father, thank You for the gift of family and the beautiful memories we create together. May we treasure these moments and share Your love through our time spent with one another.

Each Christmas memory is a thread in the tapestry of our family's love.

THE GIFT OF A FAMILY CHRISTMAS GATHERING

"Behold, how good and pleasant it is when brothers dwell in unity!"
Psalm 133:1

DEVOTIONAL

Life is not measured by how flawless our gatherings are, but by the warmth of the connections we nurture.

What special memories do you cherish from past Christmas gatherings with your family, and how can you create new ones this year?

PRAYER

Dear Lord, we thank You for the gift of family, especially during this blessed season. Help us to embrace every moment together, filling our hearts with love, joy, and gratitude.

Home is not a place, but a feeling shared with those we love.

THE JOY OF A FAMILY CHRISTMAS OUTING

"This is the day which the Lord hath made;
we will rejoice and be glad in it." **Psalm 118:24**

DEVOTIONAL

Nothing can fill a grandmother's heart quite like watching her family create memories together.

What does the joy of a family Christmas outing mean to you, and how does it remind you of the love that surrounds you during this special season?

PRAYER

Dear Lord, thank You for the gift of family and the blessings of togetherness during this Christmas season. May our hearts be filled with joy as we create cherished memories with loved ones.

Joy blooms in the hearts that gather to share life's moments, especially during the festive season.

THE BLESSING OF A FAMILY CHRISTMAS GIFT

"Beloved, I pray that all may go well with you and that you may be in good health, as it goes well with your soul." 3 John 1:2

DEVOTIONAL

This Christmas, let's cherish the gift of family, for the memories we create are everlasting treasures woven into our hearts.

What memories do you cherish the most about your family's Christmas celebrations, and how can you share those blessings with your loved ones this year?

PRAYER

Dear Lord, thank you for the gift of family and the love that binds us together during this special season. Help us to create precious memories that reflect Your love and grace.

Family is the greatest gift of all; each embrace is a blessing, each laugh a reminder of God's grace.

THE GIFT OF A FAMILY CHRISTMAS CAROL

"Let the little children come to me, and do not hinder them, for to such belongs the kingdom of God." Mark 10:14

DEVOTIONAL

The greatest gift we can give our family is the joy of togetherness, instilling in them the harmony of love and faith that resonates through generations.

What is your favorite family memory tied to a Christmas carol, and how does it remind you of the blessings of togetherness?

PRAYER

Dear God, thank you for the gift of family and the joy our voices create together during the holiday season. May our hearts be filled with love as we share the songs that carry our memories.

Every note sung together weaves a thread of love that binds our hearts during the festive season.

THE POWER OF A FAMILY CHRISTMAS BLESSING

"The Lord bless you and keep you; the Lord make his face shine upon you and be gracious to you." **Numbers 6:24-25**

DEVOTIONAL

Family is where love flourishes and blessings are recognized; by sharing them, we create cherished memories that bind us closer together.

What traditions do you cherish most during the Christmas season, and how can you share a special blessing with your family this year?

PRAYER

Dear God, as we gather our family for Christmas, may Your love fill our hearts. Bless our time together and the words we share, so that we may strengthen our bonds in faith and joy.

Family is the heart of Christmas,
where love is shared and blessings bloom.

DECEMBER 14

THE BLESSING OF A FAMILY CHRISTMAS REFLECTION

"She will give birth to a son, and you are to give him the name Jesus, because he will save his people from their sins." **Matthew 1:21**

DEVOTIONAL

In the quiet moments of reflection, remember that the essence of Christmas lies not in the gifts we give, but in the love we share with those we hold dear.

What are some special memories you cherish from past family Christmases, and how can you create new moments to celebrate this season together?

PRAYER

Dear Lord, thank you for the gift of family. As we gather this Christmas, fill our hearts with love and joy, and help us to create beautiful memories together.

Home is where the heart is, and during Christmas,
our hearts gather around the warmth of family.

DECEMBER 15

PREPARING OUR HEARTS FOR CHRIST'S ARRIVAL

"But the angel said to them, 'Do not be afraid. I bring you good news that will cause great joy for all the people. Today in the town of David, a Savior has been born to you; he is the Messiah, the Lord." Luke 2:10-11

DEVOTIONAL

Prepare your heart for Christ's coming, allowing His love to enrich your everyday moments with family and friends."

What does it mean for you to prepare your heart for Christ's arrival during this special season, and how can you share that journey with your loved ones?

PRAYER

Dear Lord, as we embrace the season of Advent, help us to cultivate our hearts and minds to welcome Your presence. May we be filled with joy and peace as we await Your coming into our lives and our families.

Just as the earth prepares for the spring, so too must our hearts be ready to bloom with love and grace at Christ's arrival.

DECEMBER 16

THE JOY OF A FAMILY CHRISTMAS MORNING

"The Lord has done great things for us, and we are filled with joy."
Psalm 126:3

DEVOTIONAL

Christmas morning teaches us that joy multiplies when shared; creating cherished memories with our family is a treasure that lasts a lifetime.

What is your favorite memory of Christmas morning with your family, and how does it bring you joy to see the next generation celebrate together?

PRAYER

Dear Lord, thank You for the gift of family and the joy that fills our hearts on Christmas morning. May we cherish these moments and reflect Your love in our gatherings.

Family gathered together is the greatest gift we can unwrap on Christmas morning.

Near the End of Our Journey

You have spent many days reflecting through these devotionals.

If this book has supported your spiritual journey, sharing a short review on Amazon helps more women discover these pages of encouragement.

devo.anchoredgraces.com/grandma

Your story may be the reason another woman finds hope.

DECEMBER 17

THE BLESSING OF A FAMILY CHRISTMAS DINNER

"The steadfast love of the Lord never ceases; his mercies never come to an end; they are new every morning; great is your faithfulness."
Lamentations 3:22-23

DEVOTIONAL

Cherish the moments spent with loved ones around the table, for in these gatherings, the truest blessings of family are revealed.

What memories do you cherish most from past family Christmas dinners, and how can you create new moments of joy this year with your loved ones?

PRAYER

Dear Lord, thank you for the gift of family and the joy of gathering together. May this Christmas dinner be filled with laughter, love, and the warmth of your presence.

Family is the heart of the holiday season,
where love and laughter weave cherished memories.

DECEMBER 18

THE GIFT OF A FAMILY CHRISTMAS STORY

"Behold, I will send you Elijah the prophet before the great and awesome day of the Lord comes. And he will turn the hearts of fathers to their children and the hearts of children to their fathers." **Malachi 4:5-6**

DEVOTIONAL

Every story passed down is a thread that weaves
our family tapestry closer together.

What treasured memories do you hold of Christmases past with your family, and how might you share those stories to inspire the younger generations?

PRAYER

Dear Lord, thank You for the gift of family and the beautiful stories that bind us together. Help us to cherish and share these memories, creating warmth and joy in our hearts this Christmas.

Every family story is a thread in the tapestry of love
that warms our hearts.

DECEMBER 19

THE POWER OF A FAMILY CHRISTMAS TRADITION

"See that you do not despise one of these little ones. For I tell you that their angels in heaven always see the face of my Father in heaven."
Matthew 18:10

DEVOTIONAL

Traditions bind our families together, nurturing love, memories, and the spirit of Christmas across generations.

What family traditions bring warmth to your Christmas celebrations? How can you pass down your cherished memories to the younger generations?

PRAYER

Dear Lord, thank you for the gift of family and the joy they bring during this special season. May our hearts be filled with love as we share stories that unite and inspire us.

Every family's story is a thread woven into the tapestry of love.

DECEMBER 20

FINDING WONDER IN THE CHRISTMAS STORY

"And the Word became flesh and dwelt among us, full of grace and truth; we have seen His glory, glory as of the only Son from the Father."
John 1:14

DEVOTIONAL

Every Christmas is a new opportunity to find joy and wonder in the smallest moments of grace that come our way.

What part of the Christmas story brings you the most joy or wonder, and how can you share that feeling with your family this season?

PRAYER

Dear Lord, thank You for the gift of Your Son and the wonder of the Christmas story. Help us to behold the beauty around us and to share it with loved ones.

In the simplicity of the nativity, we find the profound:
love wrapped in swaddling clothes.

DECEMBER 21

THE GIFT OF A FAMILY CHRISTMAS ADVENTURE

"When they saw the star, they rejoiced with exceeding great joy."
Matthew 2:10

DEVOTIONAL

Cherish the moments spent with family, for they weave the tapestry of joy
and love that lasts a lifetime.

*What traditions does your family cherish during the Christmas season, and how
might you be inspired to create new memories together this year?*

PRAYER

Dear Heavenly Father, thank You for the gift of family and the joy of our
Christmas adventures. May this season be filled with love, laughter, and
cherished moments as we gather together.

Family is the heart of Christmas,
where memories are created and love is shared.

DECEMBER 22

THE JOY OF A FAMILY CHRISTMAS BLESSING

"I will refresh the weary and satisfy the faint."
Jeremiah 31:25

DEVOTIONAL

Family is the greatest gift, and the times we share are the threads that
weave our hearts together.

*What special memories come to mind when you think of Christmas celebrations
with your family? How can you bring those joyful moments into this year's
festivities?*

PRAYER

Dear Lord, thank You for the gift of family and the joy they bring into our
lives. As we gather this Christmas, may our hearts be filled with love,
laughter, and the warmth of Your presence.

Family is the heart of Christmas, where joy and love
are wrapped in every shared moment.

DECEMBER 23

SAVORING MOMENTS OF PEACE AT CHRISTMAS

"You will keep in perfect peace those whose minds are steadfast because they trust in you." Isaiah 26:3

DEVOTIONAL

The greatest gift you can give this Christmas is not in what you accomplish but in the peace you nurture within, sharing it with those you love.

What small moments of peace can you create for yourself amidst the holiday bustle, and how can they help you connect more deeply with the spirit of Christmas?

PRAYER

Dear Lord, in this bustling season, help me to find and cherish the moments of peace that bring joy to my heart. May I be reminded of your love and the beauty that surrounds me. Amen.

Peace is not found in the absence of chaos, but in the quiet moments we carve out in its midst.

DECEMBER 24

WELCOMING THE SAVIOR

"But the angel said to them, 'Do not be afraid. I bring you good news that will cause great joy for all the people. Today in the town of David a Savior has been born to you; he is the Messiah, the Lord.'" Luke 2:10-11

DEVOTIONAL

This Christmas Eve, let us remember to invite Jesus into our hearts and homes, spreading His light to all generations.

What does it feel like for you to open your heart to the coming of the Savior this Christmas Eve? How can you create a space for His peace and love in your home and heart?

PRAYER

Dear Lord, as we gather to celebrate the birth of Your Son, fill our hearts with joy and our homes with love. Help us to embrace this holy night with open arms and welcoming hearts.

Christmas Eve is not just a night of celebration; it's an invitation to experience the warmth of His presence.

CELEBRATING CHRIST'S BIRTH

"Glory to God in the highest, and on earth peace, goodwill toward men."
Luke 2:14

DEVOTIONAL
Each time we share the Christmas story, we weave a thread of faith and love that binds generations together.

What memories from your past Christmases fill your heart with joy and remind you of Christ's love? How can you share that love with others this year?

PRAYER
Dear Lord, thank You for the gift of Your Son, Jesus, who brings hope and joy to our lives. Help us to celebrate His birth with open hearts and share that warmth with our family and friends.

Every Christmas light we see reflects the brightness of His love within us.

DECEMBER 26

THE GIFT OF A FAMILY CHRISTMAS REFLECTION

"For where your treasure is, there your heart will be also."
Matthew 6:21

DEVOTIONAL
Family is the most precious gift we can share during Christmas, nurturing love and cherishing each other in every season of life.

What does Christmas mean to you as you gather with your family, and how can you cherish these moments even more deeply this year?

PRAYER
Dear Lord, thank You for the gift of family and the love we share. Help us to embrace each moment together this Christmas, filling our hearts with joy and gratitude.

Family is the heart of Christmas, echoing love and laughter through every cherished moment.

DECEMBER 27

SHARING CHRIST'S LIGHT WITH OTHERS

"When Jesus spoke again to the people, he said, 'I am the light of the world. Whoever follows me will never walk in darkness, but will have the light of life." John 8:12

DEVOTIONAL

We may never know how far our light can reach, but sharing it with those we love is a beautiful way to illuminate their lives.

What small ways can you share Christ's light in your daily interactions with family and friends? Think about moments when your smile, a kind word, or a listening ear could reflect His love.

PRAYER

Dear Heavenly Father, thank You for the light of Your Son, Jesus. Help me to shine brightly in my family and community, spreading kindness and love in every encounter.

Even the smallest act of love can illuminate
the darkest corners of someone's heart.

DECEMBER 28

PASSING DOWN CHRISTMAS TRADITIONS

"We will not hide them from their children, but tell to the coming generation the glorious deeds of the Lord, and His might, and the wonders that He has done." Psalm 78:4

DEVOTIONAL

Every recipe and story you share with your grandchildren is a thread in the fabric of their lives, weaving love and connection across generations.

What cherished Christmas traditions do you hope to pass down to your grandchildren, and how can you invite them into these special moments this year?

PRAYER

Dear Lord, thank You for the gift of family and the memories we create together. Help me nurture these traditions, so they may continue to bring warmth and joy to generations to come.

Traditions are the threads that weave our family's story together.

THE GIFT OF A FAMILY CHRISTMAS TRADITION

"The living, the living—they praise you, as I am doing today; parents tell their children about your faithfulness." Isaiah 38:19

DEVOTIONAL

As we establish and nurture family traditions, we create a legacy of faith and love that endures through time.

What cherished Christmas traditions do you hold dear, and how can you share those special moments with your grandchildren this year?

PRAYER

Dear Lord, thank You for the joy of family and the opportunity to create lasting memories. Help me to nurture these traditions with love and wisdom as I share the magic of Christmas with my grandchildren.

Traditions are the threads that knit our hearts
together across generations.

DECEMBER 30

THE JOY OF A FAMILY CHRISTMAS REFLECTION

"The Lord your God is with you, the Mighty Warrior who saves. He will take great delight in you; in his love, he will no longer rebuke you, but will rejoice over you with singing." Zephaniah 3:17

DEVOTIONAL

Family gatherings during Christmas remind us that love is what truly makes the season bright.

What are the little moments during the holidays that fill your heart with joy and remind you of the love that binds your family together?

PRAYER

Dear Lord, thank You for the gift of family and the cherished memories of Christmas. May we embrace each moment with love and gratitude this season.

Joy is found in the gathering, in the laughter shared,
and in the warmth of togetherness.

DECEMBER 31

LOOKING BACK WITH GRATITUDE

"Even to your old age and gray hairs I am he, I am he who will sustain you. I have made you and I will carry you; I will sustain you and I will rescue you." Isaiah 46:4

DEVOTIONAL

Our memories are treasures; reflecting on them can reveal God's sustaining grace throughout our lives.

What memories come to mind when you think of moments that have filled your heart with gratitude? Who or what in your life has shaped you in ways you never expected?

PRAYER

Dear Lord, thank you for the tapestry of experiences that have woven my life together. Help me to cherish each thread of memory with gratitude and grace. May my heart overflow with thankfulness as I recognize your hand in every moment.

Gratitude is the memory of the heart.

More Devotionals from Anchored Grace

If this devotional encouraged your heart, you may also enjoy these devotionals from Anchored Grace.

- 365 Day Devotional for Women
- 90 Day Devotional for Women Seeking Peace
- 90 Day Devotional for Women Facing Anxiety and Stress
- 90 Day Devotional for Women 50+
- Guided Prayer Journal for Women

Search **"Anchored Grace Devotional"** on Amazon to discover more devotionals designed to support your journey of faith.

Thank You
for Walking This Journey

Thank you for spending this devotional journey with Anchored Grace.

If this devotional encouraged your heart, strengthened your faith, or brought peace to your daily routine, would you consider leaving a short review on Amazon?

devo.anchoredgraces.com/grandma

Reviews help other women discover devotionals that may support them through their own seasons of life.

Even a single sentence about your experience can make a difference.

We are grateful you chose Anchored Grace.

www.ingramcontent.com/pod-product-compliance
Lightning Source LLC
Chambersburg PA
CBHW071738120626
46550CB00002B/566